From Poverty to Prosperity

NKANU O. NKANU

Copyright © 2015 Nkanu O. Nkanu

All rights reserved.

No portion of this book may be reproduced, stored in a retrieval system or transmitted in any form or by any means without permission in writing from the copyright holders.

ISBN: 1976029929
ISBN-13: 978-1976029929

Unless otherwise indicated, all Bible quotations are taken from New King James Version (NKJV).

DEDICATION

To my wife, Neji and wonderful parents Mr./Mrs. Benson O. Nkanu.

ACKNOWLEDGEMENT

I am especially indebted to God's Servants such as Mike Murdock, Bishop David Oyedepo, Apostle Johnson Suleman, Bishop T.D. Jakes, Kenneth Copeland and Sunday Adelaja to mention a few, whose insightful teachings, preaching and writings have positively affected me. I have quoted very brief excerpts from some of their writings and preaching. I remain grateful to them and pray God's continuous blessings on their ministries.

Preface

Beloved of God, I congratulate you for even picking up this book. This work is a sure tool to drastically transform your life. I know this book will mightily enrich and empower you. It will surely not leave you where it found you. The book from poverty to prosperity shows you how to journey from lack to abundance.

As a student of prosperity, I have discovered that wealth isn't a miracle. Wealth is created and there are valid scriptural principles to wealth creation. This is what this book promises to deliver to you.

This book is written in parts and each part contains several chapters. Part one deals with what poverty is, its ungodly nature, the pain of poverty and reasons for poverty. Part two deals with the warfare dimension of poverty with salient mysteries that will keep you spiritually alert. Part three deals with knowing certain basics that transports you from poverty to prosperity. The fourth part includes chapters that define prosperity and its godly nature as well as biblical reasons, laws and conditions for prosperity. The fifth part is basically the conclusion of this book and it opens up your true financial status in Christ.

Each chapter in this book is a must read. It will greatly enrich your life and bring an undeniable turn around in your finances. Please understand that outside the Bible, no book contains all you need to know about wealth creation. Every book on wealth creation adds to or modifies existing laws to suit the time and location. This book in your hand contains valid biblical laws to create for you a financial throne where ever you are located.

I encourage you to read this book with an open heart and be ready to put into practice the principles of wealth creation found in the various chapters. Take it and use it as your wealth creation manual.

Let's begin.

INTRODUCTION

Life is a journey that starts at birth. The time you have spent in life is measured by your age. When Pharaoh asked Jacob how old he was, Jacob directed his attention to the fact that life is a journey. This is how I know:

Pharaoh said to Jacob, how old are you? And Jacob said to Pharaoh, the days of the years of my pilgrimage are one hundred and thirty years... and they have not attained to the days of the years of the life of my fathers in the days of their pilgrimage Genesis 47: 8, 9.

In life you are progressing, retrogressing or stagnant. One major characteristics of life is growth. Whatever does not grow dies. This is applicable to every facet of life. How old you are is not what determines your success but how well you live and the level of God given grounds you have covered. The grounds you have covered all over your time on earth, explains your speed. God wants you on the speed lane. God wants you to make speedy progress in your life's pursuit. He wants you financially successful. No single person was born rich. We all were born naked. Man becomes rich by Christ's grace plus his own conscious efforts. We all move from poverty to prosperity or the other way round. Jesus was born in the poorest place (manger) but in John fourteen He announced to His disciples a city made of mansions. It's a journey you must undertake; else you live and die poor. But this is not God's will for your life. He hates to see you stranded. He does not support those who desire to jump but He encourages those who are willing to play by the Kingdom rules and grow. Whoever jumps lacks a base and will fall by gravity; but those who grow have a solid foundation and they shall abide.

The will of God for every Christian is prosperity (3John 1: 2). 2 Corinthians 8: 9 reveals that Christ was rich, yet for our sakes He became poor, that we through His poverty might become rich. So in simple sense: **He became poor so we might become rich.** Remember that the scripture cannot be broken (John 10: 35). So where do we now place poor Christians? Why are many Christians poor and beggarly? Is there something these folks are not doing well? Do you know that some ignorant people even feel that Christianity is a religion for the poor? No! The God we serve is the most successful individual in the whole universe. He owns everything in the whole wide world (Psalm 24: 1). If your father (God) is rich and you are His heir, then that poverty in your life is a terrible error that this book in your hand has come to eradicate.

Read this book with a teachable heart and be prepared to apply the biblical principles therein. It will transport you from the realm of poverty to prosperity. If you are ready to grow into a financial warlord, ride with me.

CONTENTS

	Dedication	iii
	Acknowledgments	iv
	Preface	
	Introduction	
1	What Is Poverty?	1
2	Is Poverty Godly?	Pg 5
3	The Pain of Poverty	Pg 9
4	Reasons for Poverty	Pg 14
5	There Is More to Poverty	Pg 25
6	The Nonsense Must Stop	Pg 28
7	Stop Them or They Will Stop You	Pg 35
8	Destroying Attackers of Seeds	Pg 37
9	The Power of What You Know	Pg 42
10	Money	Pg 44
11	Secrets of the Prosperous	Pg 52
12	Success	Pg 55
13	Planning	Pg 65
14	Ideas	Pg 69
15	What Is Prosperity?	Pg 74
16	Prosperity Is Godly	Pg 75
17	Why God Prospers His People	Pg 80

18	Conditions for Prosperity	Pg 87
19	Your True Financial Status in Christ	Pg 108

CHAPTER ONE

WHAT IS POVERTY?

Poverty is the state of having very little or no money; not having enough money for basic needs such as food, shelter, clothing and education etc. The poor are those who live at the mercy of the rich and comfortable. The poor are those deserving pity and sympathy. They are those who are low or lower than expected in status. They are very unskilled in wealth creation. Their resource base is extremely low. Sunday Adelaja in his book **"Money won't make you rich"** came up with a shocking revelation that five percent of the world's population is controlling ninety-five percent of the wealth of the world while the remaining five percent is shared by ninety-five percent of the world's population. His reason is not farfetched; he posited that this five percent controlling world's resource base know the law of money and are skilled in wealth creation while the vast percentage of the world's population do not. The poor are like countries void of resources and soils void of nutrients. They lack good quality and characteristics.

The following words are used in describing the poor:

Disadvantaged: This is used to refer to those having less money and fewer opportunities than most people in society. Money creates opportunities. When you lack money, you are starved of opportunities but when you have it, you select opportunities. The reason for most missed opportunities in life is because of lack of money. When there is money in your hand, opportunities to own lands, houses, cars, travel and be a blessing are at your beck and call.

Needy: These are the poor considered as a group

Impoverished: This term is used to talk about poor countries and the people who live there. There are people in life who get rich by making others poor. The book of Judges 6: 6 reveals that Israel was greatly impoverished by the Midianites. The poverty of many people in the world is both directly and indirectly caused by certain others who gain greatly from their predicaments. The passage below revealed the plight of Israel who suffered greatly because their ration was being enjoyed by a stronger nation called Midian.

So Israel was greatly impoverished because of the Midianites...Judges 6: 6

Deprived: They are those without enough food, education and all the things that are necessary for the people to live a happy and comfortable life. This term is used for poor areas in rich countries. These sorts are living in the midst of plenty but experiencing penury. Their situation is like the proverbial sailor who in the midst of the high sea was thirsty, who thus exclaimed, "water everywhere but non to drink". The deprived are likened to the lamed man in Acts chapter 3, sitting at the beautiful gate but with ugly experiences and Mordecai, a gate man in the palace where his niece sat on the throne as queen. This error must be corrected in the name of Jesus. The deprived are robbed of comfort in the midst of abundance.

The profit of the land is for all; even the king is served from the field Eccl. 5: 9

If it is for all, then you don't have any reason to be poor, your background notwithstanding. Stop that demon of infirmity trying to deprive you of your provision.

You prepare a table before me in the presence of my enemies; you anoint my head with oil, my cup runs over Psalm 23: 5

Your enemies cannot take your provision because the oil that will make you outshine them has been released upon you. Stop being deprived. The enemy is the one at your mercy.

...oil to make his head shine, and bread which strengthens man's heart Psalm 104: 15

You need that living bread to strengthen yourself and to rule in the midst of your enemies

I am the bread of life

This is the bread which comes down from heaven...

I am the living bread which comes from heaven... John 7: 48, 50, 51

It is your season to reign. No more deprivation. Whatever you were deprived of in time passed, the living bread, the rod of your strength is restoring back to you.

The Lord shall send the rod of your strength out of Zion. Rule in the midst your enemies! Psalm 110: 2

Hard up: This refers to those having very little money, especially for a short period of time.

Poverty-Stricken: This means to be extremely poor. When poverty gets to the point where even the poor call you poor, you know you need to do more to secure divine attention. When your condition has gotten to the point where even the poor see and pity your existence, it means you are poverty-stricken.

In the Christendom, over 70 per cent of believers are below poverty line; that is the estimated minimum level of income needed to secure the necessities of life. The reason for this is the prevalent religious dogma taught. Many Christians believe it is sinful and dangerous to be wealthy since the Bible says it will be easier for the camel to go through the eye of a needle than for a rich person to enter the kingdom of God. Listen! This statement is related to those who are ruled by the love of money. You can be poverty-stricken and still be possessed with the love of money. Greed operates in both the rich and the poor. God is in favor of prosperity. I shall be showing you that in the subsequent chapters of this book. I refuse to go to heaven poor like Lazarus. I choose to be rich and make heaven like father Abraham. That way I can lay up treasures above.

It is important you also know that if you have enough for yourself and family alone with nothing to extend to others, you are still poor. You are operating on a subsistence level. You are only prosperous when you are a blessing. You are blessed to finance the gospel and to reach out to others. God's will for you is that you should have enough to the overflow so that everyone in your family is satisfied, and then enough to help others and also to finance the great commission. Until you get to this point, you are still poor. If you are stingy, finding it very hard to release to someone, you are poor. If you are selfish, robbing others (including God) to please yourself, you are poor. If there is just one car in the house for you to drive and non for your wife and children's use, you are still poor. Don't be satisfied with that level. It is still poverty. When God called you, He had greatness on His mind. He wants you better than this level because your new birth placed you in the god class. You are better than this. You are better than where you are living, what you are eating, the money you are earning, what you are wearing and what you are doing.

Prosperity in God starts at new birth. To prosper in God means to prosper first in your soul (the mind realm which houses your will and emotions), then your body must be healthy and then material possessions. If any of these is out of place, you are still poor. If you are rich in possession but are not born again or are oppressed with illness, you are still poor. Read this book with an open heart because the Holy Spirit will grant you all you need to move to the next level of your life. I see a season of abundance coming on you in Jesus precious Name.

CHAPTER TWO

IS POVERTY GODLY?

There is nothing godly about poverty. Poverty does not make you look like God. God is the richest and most successful individual in the whole universe. The heavens and earth belongs to Him. Revelation 21 reveals a gold city owned by God. Jesus in John 14: 2 revealed to us a kingdom filled with mansions. In Haggai 2: 8 the Lord announced thus *"the silver is mine, the gold is mine..."* This should tell you that your heavenly Father is a rich God. He owns the heavens, the earth and the entire water body. How can your heavenly Father be rich and you are poor, broke and beggarly? He is not a wicked Father. It is a grave error to be called the poor son of a rich Father. That error must be corrected by fire in the name of Jesus. There is nothing godly about poverty. Hear what the prodigal son said:

...how many of my father's hired servants have bread enough and to spare (prosperity), and I perish with hunger (poverty)! I will arise and go to my father...Luke 15: 17, 18

It is time to arise and go to your God. He has enough and to spare in stock for you. He is waiting for you to take action. Until you take action poverty will not cease dressing you with rags. Poverty corrupts your beauty and this is the first thing the Father intends to address in your life.

But the father said to his servants, bring out the best robe and put it on him, and put a ring on his hand and sandals on his feet Luke 15: 22

Poverty is not good for you because it compels you to change your diet. Poverty feeds you with meals meant for swine and dogs. But God wants to correct that and give you your right diet.

...bring the fatted calf here and kill it, and let us eat and be merry Luke 15:23

It is not poverty that qualifies you for heaven but purity. In fact poverty is a threat to your heavenly vision because it can tempt you to steal, envy others or do something unpleasant against God. The poor who by God's grace make heaven may find it had to adapt to his new environment (my way of amusing my audience). You must know that poverty is a function of choice. The word says:

The poor will never cease from the land... Deut. 15: 11

Jesus also posited in Matthew 26 verse 11 that the poor will always be around, but I cannot find where your name was mentioned to be the poor one. You only become poor when you choose to. To live or die, be rich or poor, become an asset or liability, is a function of the decision you make.

I call heaven and earth as witnesses today against you, that I have set before you life and death, blessing and cursing; therefore choose life, that both you and your descendants may live Deut. 30: 19

So you see that what you become is a function of what you choose. The choice you make will affect your posterity positively or negatively. You have been advised on the choice to make:

...choose life...Deut. 30: 19

Choose life; choose blessing and make your descendants happy. Good parents leave inheritance for not just their children but grand children. Poverty is an abuse to the work of grace.

For you know the grace of our Lord Jesus Christ, that though He was rich, yet for your sakes, He became poor, that you through His poverty might become rich 2Corithians 8: 9

And that He might make known the riches of His glory on the vessels of mercy, which He had prepared beforehand for glory Romans 9:23

...Christ in you, the hope of glory Col. 1:27

In death, Christ took our place of hopelessness, poverty and deprivation and in resurrection, He conveyed us into His kingdom (the city of gold) Col. 1: 13. To be poor is to abuse the work of atonement; the work of substitution that Jesus did for us. It grieves Christ to see a believer living in poverty. You are His ambassador here on earth and how you live and appear paints a picture of the personality and kingdom you represent. It will be a big shame to America for their ambassador to look tattered and battered as he represents her in Nigeria. As long as her ambassador remain connected, stick to their laws and go about his mission in Nigeria, he will continue enjoying the protection and provision of his country. Strike, inflation, scarcity of resources does not affect his upkeep because; his supply comes from America (his source). This is the same with a Christian; our source is God. He is our **'abba'** meaning source. As long as we remain connected to Him and observe to do His commands, we will enjoy abundance even in the midst of scarcity.

Poverty is not a sin but a curse brought by sin. Christ became accursed to release the Abrahamic blessing on us. A poor Christian will still make heaven if he remains holy and faithful to God. We know this because of Lazarus. But you may not have treasures laid up in heaven. You lay up treasures in heaven through your giving on earth. Don't be like Lazarus who the bible says is in Abraham's bosom. A poor man will have nothing to give so as to lay up treasures in heaven. Poverty is not good for you. It is not godly to be poor. If God wanted you poor then He would not have created Adam and put him in the Garden of Eden, a place of abundance. Poverty is the byproduct of the curse. Sin brought the effect of the curse. Adam and Eve lived in abundance until they sinned and were driven from the place of rest to the place of stress. Jesus changed that when He came and died for us all. You are not permitted to be poor again. Arise and shine.

Poverty does not spread the gospel. Poverty closes up mission fields and slows the execution of the great commission since you need money to send missionaries to the field, sponsor television and radio programs, print Bibles and tracts etc. Prosperity spreads the gospel faster than you can imagine.

Poverty is a terrible weight. It slows the speed of its victim. You cannot be carrying a heavy substance and expect to finish a race early. You will always arrive late. Poverty gives its victim the snail speed. Hebrews 12: 1 commands that us to

...lay aside every weight...

I therefore recommend prosperity. It will give you the speed you never imagined. You need a radical restoration. You shall arrive early. Pray with me now.

Prayer Point: oh Lord my Father, visit me early.

CHAPTER THREE

THE PAIN OF POVERTY

Poverty has done a lot of havoc. I hate poverty with every fiber of my being and I dare to announce to you that it is enough. There is nothing good about poverty. All I see in it is harm. It is not good for you. Poverty is the reason for most untimely deaths, stress, hypertension, name them. It is the reason for uncompleted projects, unexecuted visions, malnutrition, sicknesses and diseases, increased crime wave etc. One demonic spirit that is enlarging poverty in the developing countries is corruption and if something drastic is not done, it will grow worse. Pray with me.

Prayer Point: In the name of Jesus Christ I paralyze corruption in the land

55 scriptural facts about the wickedness of poverty

- The poor is void of confidence
- Poverty slows your speed
- It is the reason for many untimely deaths. Lazarus is an example. Most people who die in hospitals died because of poverty. Malnutrition resulting to sickness, diseases and deaths are caused by poverty.
- Poverty brings shame and reproach
- The poor suffer oppression Eccl. 5: 8
- The poor is stripped of possession. He has nothing 2 Samuel 12: 3

- They are object of oppression and abandonment Job 20: 19
- The poor are prone to murder Job 24: 14
- They are sorrowful people Job 34: 28, Psalm 69: 29
- A poor man's wisdom is often despised Eccl. 9: 16
- A poor man's words are not heard Eccl. 9: 10
- They are object of affliction Job 36:15
- The poor suffer persecution Psalm 10: 2; 109: 16
- They are subject to attack Psalm 10: 8
- The counsel of the poor is shamed Psalm 14: 6
- The poor are plundered by the strong Psalm 35: 10; Mark 4: 25
- The poor is constantly in need Psalm 86: 1
- Poverty brings destruction Isaiah 32: 7. How would a normal person be comfortable with a destroyer? Destroy poverty before it destroys your destiny and that of your descendants.
- The poor do not hear rebuke Prov. 13: 8
- The poor attracts hatred easily Prov. 14: 20. People don't like identifying with failure but they crowd around success. Poverty makes you a lone ranger. Do something about your life.
- A poor man is hardly remembered Eccl. 9: 15
- They are object of mockery Prov. 17: 5
- The poor lack confidence and also beg Prov. 17:5
- Poverty separates its victims from their friends Prov. 19: 4
- The poor are under the control of the rich Prov. 22: 7
- Poverty turns people to borrowers Prov. 22: 7. It is not God's will for you to borrow but He wills that you lend to nations (Deut. 28: 12)
- The poor are often robbed and deprived Prov. 22: 22; Isaiah 3: 14
- They are object of pity Prov. 28: 8
- They are recipients of the cruelty of the wicked Prov. 28: 15
- Most poor people are regularly tempted to steal Prov. 30: 19
- They are prey to devourers Prov. 30: 14
- A poor man's face is grinded Isaiah 3: 15

- Poverty alters one's identity. It precedes your name Isaiah 10: 30 (Poor Anathoth). It changed the prodigal son from a prince to a slave.
- The poor suffer from thirst and hunger. Poverty reduces your taste. Lazarus preferred crumbs instead of the main meal (Luke 16: 20, 21); the prodigal son ate with swine. Poverty debases. Get rid of it. You don't belong there.
- Poverty makes one an outcast Isaiah 58: 7
- Poverty dresses her victims with rags and strips them of beauty. The face of a poverty-stricken person is hardly attractive. Poverty steals your smile.
- Many are homeless because of poverty. In Lagos you find people sleeping under bridges because of lack of money to buy or rent accommodation
- Poverty is the reason for malnutrition and consequent diseases and deaths
- Poverty exposes people to untimely death Jeremiah 2: 34
- Poverty turns many to liabilities 1Cor. 13:3
- They are oppressed, robbed and mistreated Ezekiel 22: 29
- The poor are treated as commoners and sold for worthless prices Amos 2: 6
- They are tread down Amos 5: 11
- They are easily diverted from the cause of justice Amos 5: 12
- They are prone to failures Amos 5: 4
- The destiny of the poor is easily bought Amos 5: 6. If Esau had his own food or money, he wouldn't have sold his birthright for a plate of pottage
- The wicked feast on the poor in secret places Hab. 3: 14. The dogs feasted on the wounds of Lazarus until he died (Luke 16: 21, 22). The wicked today, both those on the throne and many others around are feasting and getting fat from the weaknesses of the poor. The poor are getting poorer and having access to unstandardized schools while the wicked are stealing the money meant for development and are enjoying it with their children who are schooling in the best schools within and outside the country. How long will this evil continue? Pray with me

Prayer Point: 1. anyone prospering through my weakness, expire in Jesus Name **2.** Whoever is living comfortably from my discomfort, expire in Jesus Name **3.** Anyone excelling because of my suffering die in Jesus Name

It will not continue like this; no longer shall the dogs feast on your weakness again. You won't die like Lazarus. You cannot die because of dogs. They will die your death in the name of Jesus. Shout fire like thunder.

- Poverty has vowed never to be without prisoners Deut. 15: 11; Matt. 26: 11
- Poverty makes you a depend ant Matt. 19: 21; 26: 9; Mark 10: 21
- The poor is constantly in lack. He is at the mercy of people (Rom. 15: 26). You don't need to always collect from people. It is dangerous. There are cases of people whose destinies were bought by certain wicked fellows who gave them gifts. Until you break free from the firm grip of these satanic agents, you will continue to work for them to enjoy. Pray this

Prayer Point: Every firm grip of the wicked on my destiny; I am not your slave, therefore break by the reason of the anointing in the name of Jesus Christ.

- The poor remain in suffering, until they are remembered Galatians 2: 10. Pray with me: Oh Lord, send my helper. Your distance from where you are to the place of your prosperity is a man.
- The reason for filthy clothes is poverty James 2: 2
- Poverty activates disrespect and debasement James 2: 3
- Poverty brings dishonor James 2: 6
- A poor man has no relations because he is deserted. No one loves to identify with failure. Lazarus at the rich man's gate was deserted. The impotent man at the pool called Bethesda was deserted John 5: 7

You can now see that a poor person is terribly disadvantaged. There is nothing attractive about poverty. Fight your way out of it. It is not God's will for you to be poor. He wants you to be very rich because there are a lot in your destiny to fulfill. Declare this with spiritual aggression: **Poverty I hate you and reject you today, die from your root by fire in the name of Jesus Christ. Amen.**

CHAPTER FOUR

REASONS FOR POVERTY

There are always reasons for whatever happens under the sun. The scripture which can never be broken has rightly revealed that Christ became poor so that through His poverty, we may be rich (2Cor. 8: 9). So if a Christian is not prospering, it is not the fault of God. I believe there is something the person is not doing right. Of course you cannot be doing things wrongly and expect to get correct result. You will always garbage out what you garbage in. you reap what you sow; that is Bible truth for you. So let us see some of the reasons for poverty.

POOR:

This is an acronym for the phrase **'Passing Over Opportunities Repeatedly'.** To pass over an opportunity is to lose wealth. To allow opportunities elude you continuously is to sign agreement with poverty. Opportunities are gift from God. Mike Murdock defines it as **"any situation where your favorable qualities and skills, known or unknown, can be recognized, received and ultimately rewarded"**. God is the God of opportunities. He gives men opportunities to repent, rebuild and even receive miracles. There are opportunities in every circumstance. During a terrible famine, God gave a woman of Zarephath the opportunity to use her faith and save her life and her son by giving her last meal to Elijah (1Kings 17). Opportunities are always near you, merely awaiting your recognition of them. When you allow these opportunities pass by, you lengthen your days in misery. Blind Bartimus shouted and cried unto Jesus to secure the opportunity for the restoration of his sight; the woman with the issue of blood pressed through the crowd to get her healing; Zacchius out ran the crowd and climbed up a tree to gain Christ's attention. What are you doing with opportunities? You need to recognize one when it comes, because you may never have it come around again.

Continuous Acquisition of Liabilities:

Liabilities here refer to things that constantly take money out of your hand. A man who craves and continuously acquire liabilities shall soon begin to be in want. A man who is paying to maintain his car bills, water rates, phone bills, house rent, school fees, family upkeep and other bills without assets (that which generates money) on ground will soon begin to borrow. You are advised to go for assets before liabilities and also spend wisely.

Prodigality:

When you spend without planning, you end up wasting money. The story of the prodigal son in Luke 16 teaches us to know that every waster ends up in lack. You don't waste resources and expect to be rich. God is against wastage. **Fools waste money, mediocre spend money but wise people invest money**. When Jesus fed the five thousand, He instructed His disciples to gather the remaining. Whatever you waste, you abuse and whatever you abuse will never come back to you. Wasting does not add value to your life; it rather devalues your person. Every waster will be wasted. You are advised to be prudent.

Living to Impress People:

It is believed by many that the first impression you make matter; that it goes a long way to add or subtract from you. But the truth is, no matter how well you try, you can never impress everybody. If this is so, then learn to be yourself. Live your life within the dictates of scriptural principles. Many young men have been rendered bankrupt in their bid to impress their opposite sex. Taking a girl to high class restaurants or joint that you ordinarily cannot afford just to impress her tantamount to foolishness. You don't have to be who you are not to please anyone. That is hypocrisy you know! Using your hard earn month's salary to buy a pair of shoes just to represent (as it is often said), is stupidity. The rich will create an avenue to generate more income before they buy such shoes. Looking good is very good, but plan your life first. The English entrepreneur will tell you it's business before pleasure. Before the rich buys a brand new jeep, he is sure the means to maintain it has been planned for but the poor and middle class will use all their life's savings to buy it and become stranded thereafter. Please be yourself. Plan to grow your capital base before going for certain expensive things. You can buy and use decent and affordable things until your income has grown to the point where you can buy any kind of item you desire. Don't live your life trying to impress people. It will cost you greatly and rob you of happiness. Be wise. Note this: **_fools waste money, mediocre spend money but the wise invest it to generate more money_**.

Inactivity:

Your unproductivity is a function of your inactivity. Proverbs 10: 4 says he who has a slack hand becomes poor. Proverbs 13: 23 reveal that much food is in the fallow ground of the poor. Until something is done to the ground, hunger continues. To be lazy is to invite hunger. Until there is work in your hand, God has nothing to bless. Your wealth is in your work. Proverbs 6:9-11 says how long will you slumber, o sluggard? When will you rise from your sleep? A little sleep, a little slumber, a little folding of the hands to sleep, so shall your poverty come on you like a prowler and your need like an armed man. Those who are doing nothing are possessors of poverty. Poverty is the pride possession of those who are void of profitable activity. In Proverbs 20: 13, it is re echoed thus "do not love sleep, lest you come to poverty". Sleep begets poverty. To be sleepy and lethargic will clothe you with rags (Prov. 23: 21). Paul said he who does not work should not eat. Nothing works for idle people; things only work for workers. Your work is your worth. Jesus does not want you to be idle.

...He went out and found others standing idle, and said to them, why have you been standing here idle all day?... also go into the vineyard and whatever is right you will receive Matthew 20: 6, 7

You only receive whatever is right when you engage the law of work. Work is not a curse but existed before the curse. It is work that brings worth. No jobless or lazy person is qualified for plenty. Our father of faith, Abraham was a hard worker. If Abraham's blessings must be yours, then you must do what he did to earn it. Arise and work.

Love of Pleasure:

He who loves pleasure will be a poor man... Prov. 21: 17

This refers to enjoyment and entertainment, as opposed to necessity. To love enjoyment and entertainment rather than being business minded, lands you into untold poverty. This was where the prodigal son missed it. He went all out for momentary enjoyment and satisfaction without planning to invest his money. He became broke and beggarly and later began to eat with swine. Be reasonable. The saying "business before pleasure" is the rich man's mindset. Certain fools get out of control when God permits money into their hand. Their sexual appetite automatically rises by a maximum propensity, so that they pay to sleep with several women. They even go ahead to having permanent rooms in hotels for their escapades. Be wise my friend, poverty is by the corner.

When you run a budget that is above your income

When you run an expenses schedule that consistently outweigh your income, that's poverty suffocating you. It's the poor man's mentality to live above your cash inflow. The reason for this is your inability to tame your appetite. If you always go buying things your eyes see and your heart desire when ever money comes into your hands in the bid to enjoy life, you'll end up in poverty. You must learn to control your appetite and avoid spending money on things you can do without. Save and invest such monies and you'll grow into prosperity. Grow your capital base through a conscious effort of savings and investment. It is unwise to acquire liabilities with loans all in the bid to satisfy your heart desires.

Love of Wine and Gluttony:

...he who loves wine and oil will not be rich Prov. 21: 17

For the drunkard and the glutton will come to poverty Prov. 23: 21

Pursuit of Frivolity:

...he who follows frivolity will have poverty enough Prov. 28: 19

Disobedience (Deut. 28: 15-52)

It is a dangerous thing to live in disobedience. It provokes the curse of God on your life (Deut. 28: 15).

But if you refuse and rebel, you shall be devoured by the sword, for the mouth of the Lord has spoken Isaiah 1: 20

As long as Peter stood to complain and not obey the command of Jesus to lay down his net, he remained in lack. You need to absolutely obey the principles of God for wealth creation before you can walk out on poverty. John 2: 5 says **"whatever He tells you to do, do it".** To obey commands yields more results than sacrifice.

Unredeemed Vows can slow your prosperity:

When you make vow to God, do not delay to pay it, For He has no pleasure in fools. Pay what you have vowed. Better not to vow than to vow and not pay. Do not let your mouth cause your flesh to sin, nor say before the messenger of the Lord that it was an error. Why should God be angry at your excuse and destroy the work of your hands Eccl. 5: 4- 6

Why your business is not yielding may be traced to unredeemed vows. Delays in promotion and general hardship may be because of this sin. Redeem your vows and don't be hasty to make promises you know you cannot keep. God sees those who vow and do not redeem as fools and this provokes a curse on the work of your hands. No matter what it will cost you, clear your vows, so you can earn for yourself a blessing.

Ignorance:

To be ignorant of kingdom laws does not excuse you from the hardship that offenders suffer. Ignorance is a destroyer of destiny and posterity (Hosea 4: 6).

...surely these are poor. They are foolish. For they do not know the way of the Lord Jeremiah 5: 4

The problem we see in the kingdom is that her citizens want to see the acts of God without knowing His ways. It is dangerous to seek after the acts of God without understanding His ways. This was the reason for the incessant deaths among the Israelites during their wilderness experience. It is the ways of God that provoke His acts. Moses knew the way of God, so the acts were at his beck and call. Israel was only interested in the acts and thus complained at every slightest opportunity. The scripture above reveal these guys are poor because of foolishness. They are ignorant of the way of God. You don't make headway in life until you are ready to do it God's way. Kingdom wealth can only be achieved God's way. You don't need to get wealth the way the worldly do. That is the devil's way. The word says

...do not fret because of him who prospers in his way, because of the man who brings wicked schemes to pass...do not fret-it only causes harm. For evildoers shall be cut off; but those who wait on the Lord, they shall inherit the earth. For yet a little while and the wicked shall be no more; indeed, you will look carefully for his place, but it shall be no more Psalm 37: 7-10

So you see that the way of the wicked leads to doom. Be patient with God and follow His instructions. It pays a lot. If the wicked are faithful in carrying out satanic instructions to gain fake riches, I charge you to follow after God. His blessing makes one rich and adds no sorrow at all.

He has shown you, O man, what is good; and what does the LORD require of you but to do justly, to love mercy, and to walk humbly with your God?   Micah 6: 8

Ingratitude:

To be unthankful to God is to be unreasonable. Ingratitude drains you of kingdom blessing and opens the door for curses to come in. the story of the ten lepers reveals that God loves to be appreciated. Jesus asked" were they not ten that were healed, where are the nine?" the only guy that returned with gratitude received a second touch from Jesus. Hear what God says

If you will not hear, and if you will not take it to heart, to give glory to my name; says the Lord of hosts, I will send a curse upon you and I will curse your blessings. Yes I have cursed them already because you do not take it to heart Malachi 2: 2

Ingratitude provokes the king's curse on your blessing. Every Israelite who murmured in the wilderness, all died by the curse of God. Thank God for what you have and what you don't have will be released. What gives you unhindered entrance through the king's gates is a life of thanksgiving. **We thank God for His goodness; we praise Him for His greatness and worship Him for His holiness**. Learn to thank Him always because there is grave danger in ingratitude. See this scripture:

Because you did not serve the Lord your God with joy and gladness of heart, for the abundance of everything, therefore you shall serve your enemies, whom the Lord shall send against you, IN HUNGER, IN THIRST, IN NAKEDNESS, and IN NEED OF EVERYTHING; and He will put a yoke of iron on your neck until He has destroyed you Deut. 28: 47-48

So you see from the passage that poverty (hunger, thirst, nakedness and need of everything) inhabits unthankful and unpraiseful people. Poverty is not good for you in any sense. Gratitude will provoke God's blessing (that makes rich and adds no sorrow) upon you.

Stinginess:

God is a distributor; not a collector and require His children to do same. Hence the curse of poverty is activated when you are stingy and a blessing also activated when you distribute (give to others).

There is one who makes himself rich (accumulates), yet has nothing; and one who makes himself poor (who distributes), yet has great riches Prov. 13: 7

There is one who scatters (distributes), yet increases more; and there is one who withholds (is stingy) more than is right, but it leads to poverty Prov. 11: 24

To gain riches by oppressing the poor:

He who oppresses the poor to increase his riches…will surely come to poverty Proverbs 22: 16

To disdain correction:

Poverty and shame will come to him who disdains correction…Prov. 13: 18

Refusal to commit your resources to the building of God's house:

This people say 'the time has not come, the time that the Lord's house should be built…Is it time for you yourselves to dwell in your paneled houses, and this temple lie in ruins? Haggai 1: 2-4

The consequence of this behavior is serious.

You have sown much and bring in little; you eat, but do not have enough; you drink, but you are not filled with drink; you cloth yourselves, but no one is warm; and he who earns wages, earns wages to put into a bag with holes. You look for much, but indeed it came too little; and when you brought it home, I blew it away. Why… because of my house that is in ruins while every one of you runs to his own house Haggai 1: 6, 9

Until you commit yourself to building the house of God, your venturing into abundance is at risk. Men who build God's house secure for themselves His maximum attention. When David set his heart on building for God, God established his throne; when Solomon built and sacrificed to God, he commanded God's overwhelming presence to the point that the priests ministering on the altar were unable to stand the power of the presence; the centurion built for God and compelled the attention of Christ. It is rewarding to build for God and also dangerous to hide your resources from building His house.

Defaulting in tithing and offerings:

Tithe is the foundation of your financial fulfillment. No one dares put up a structure without a solid foundation. You know that such house is bound to crash. If your tithe is not in place, you have no financial future.

If the foundations are destroyed, what can the righteous do? Psalm 11: 3

Defaulting in tithing turns God to your principal enemy. How possible is it to fight God and win? The word says

... You have robbed me...In tithes and offerings. You are cursed with a curse, for you have robbed me, even this whole nation Malachi 3: 8, 9

Get my book on tithing titled **"Tithe! Pay it or face the curse"**, for a detailed information on the subject.

Lack of Zeal amongst many to Find, Develop and Give their Gifts

Everyone in planet Earth has a special God-given talent; something you are the best at, but you have to find it. The reason so many people are below average is because finding, developing and giving ones gift is a very hard work. Most people don't actually want to work that hard. One would ordinarily think that if God has bestowed gifts on people then it should be easily accessible. The fact remains that finding, developing and giving your gift requires deliberate effort and time. Great doctors spend years in school and then practice for years developing their gift. Finding one's gift can be a hard work, and then developing one's gift can be even harder work. This is why so many people appear to be below average. This accounts for why most professional athletes practice harder than amateurs. They dedicate their life to developing their strength and skills in order to develop their gift.

These factors among several others are responsible why many Christians are still trapped in poverty. We shall deal with the solutions in the subsequent chapters.

PART TWO

The Warfare Dimension

CHAPTER FIVE

THERE IS MORE TO POVERTY

I strongly believe that there is more to poverty than meets the eyes. The devil is so afraid of prosperity in the hands of believers because he knows it is a terrible weapon to enlarge God's kingdom and depopulate his. Money in the hands of believers will spread the gospel and enlarge God's kingdom. Also the cause of Satan is advanced when money is in the hand of unbelievers. Those who control the financial atmosphere of a place also control the spiritual atmosphere to a very great extent. Satan knows this too well and that is why he is not resting at making sure that Christians go broke and beggarly.

There is a spirit behind poverty which also works with the spirit of infirmity. When the demon of infirmity gets hold of a person, it keeps him in a condition for a very long time. It most often remains, until the person dies just to make sure he does not fulfill God's purpose on earth. The impotent man at the pool of Bethesda was kept in that condition for 38years; the lamed man at the beautiful gate was held bound for 40years; the woman with the issue of blood suffered for 12years and many more. These victims and many more not mentioned were severely impoverished and some turned to beggars. But they all got their deliverance; therefore deliverance from above is coming upon you in the name of Jesus. One objective of the devil is to turn you into a beggar. That messenger of poverty oppressing your life will collide with the rock of your salvation in the name of Jesus.

In one of our meetings, I was led to move the crowd mainly youths into warfare against the spirit behind poverty. The prayer point was destroying the garment of poverty. As the congregation began praying powerfully, suddenly the atmosphere changed and these youths were collapsing under the power of God. I observed people being supernaturally delivered. This was where I decided to always do battle against the spirit behind poverty where ever I preach and also teach God's principle for prosperity. We have seen great result from this.

In Africa we know that witchcraft agents are the direct enforcers of poverty. Wherever they are found, they render the inhabitants of such circle poor. It is time to arise and fight for your life and family. Until there is warfare, there will be no welfare. Fight for your future and posterity (Neh. 4: 14). The devil is not a gentle being. You need spiritual aggression to knock him out of your way. Until he is put in his rightful place, you will not enjoy your rightful place. When he manifested in heaven, it took spiritual aggression to cast him down to earth.

And war broke out in heaven: Michael and his angels fought with the dragon and the dragon and his angels fought but they did not prevail, nor was a place found for them in heaven any longer. So the great dragon was cast out, that serpent of old, called the devil and Satan, who deceives the whole world; he was cast to the earth and his angels were cast out with him...therefore rejoice, o heaven Revelation 12: 7-9, 12

You can see that heaven rejoiced when he was cast down. Heaven did nothing until he was thrown out with his angels. His presence on earth brought woes. See this

... Woe to the inhabitants of the earth and the sea! For the devil has come down to you, having great wrath...Revelation 12: 12

So you see that until you do battle and cast him out, he stays around corrupting your inheritance. But don't worry, Jesus has conquered him and has given us power over these jokers.

... He gave them power against unclean spirits, to cast them out...Matt.10: 1

Arise and do battle for there is more to poverty than meet the eyes. Poverty is a great tool in the hands of the devil against Christians to hinder their greatness and the great commission. But he is fighting a loosed battle because Christ has promised to build His church against all odds. Heaven is releasing abundant harvest upon the believers to propagate the gospel, populating heaven and depopulating hell. Hell is about to witness loses of captives it has never experienced before. God is raising kingdom financial pillars to sponsor missionaries, embark on television and radio programs, printing bibles and tracts, organizing programs of all sorts to provoke a mass movement from the kingdom of darkness into the kingdom of God.

CHAPTER SIX

THE NONSENSE MUST STOP

There is an evil I have seen under the sun as an error proceeding from the ruler: folly is set in great dignity, while the rich sit in a lowly place. I have seen servants on horses, while princes walk on the ground as servants Eccl. 10: 5-7

There are four evils, also called errors, spotted in this passage. God called them evil because from the beginning it was not so (Matt. 19: 8). These are the errors:

Fools occupying places of prominence:

It is an error for a fool to be given staff of office. Who are these fools the bible is talking about?

The fool has said in his heart there is no God. They are corrupt, they have done abominable works, there is non who does good Psalm 14: 1

The issues of life proceed from the heart. Anyone who does not accept Christ as Lord and Savior, who is corrupt in practices, who does no good and ventures into abominable acts according to the Bible is called a fool. Power is not meant for such people. God says it is an evil and it must be corrected. The uncontrolled corrupt practices in societies today are caused by these groups of people. They have so corrupted the economy so that the resources meant for the populace are diverted into few hands. They indulge in abominable occult practices to stay in power. They are called fools in the scripture. This is God's position concerning them:

Luxury is not fitting for a fool...Proverbs 19: 10

This is true because they abuse the wealth of the masses. They promote demonic practices, venture into sexual immorality, buy sophisticated cars, and build high class houses at the expense of the masses. While the masses are groaning because of hardship, they go about living in affluence with the resources of the masses meant for development. These people go into power with the heart of servants and immediately turn into savages when they take the sit of power. The Lord shall dethrone them the same way He did to their father the devil. Those who are sponsoring corruption in Africa will experience swift judgment from the Lord of Hosts.

The rich sitting in low places:

These are those that have experienced the new birth. It is the will of God that believers should sit in prominent sits. People will always rejoice when the righteous are on the throne. Jesus through the work of grace took our poverty and made us rich (2Cor. 8: 9). If Christ has made you rich, where then is poverty coming from? It is because of the ruler (the devil). The error must be corrected. By vengeance unction there shall be a complete overturning until you (the right person) sit on the throne in Jesus name (Ezekiel 21: 27).

Prayer Point :(1) In the name of Jesus I don't belong here, I therefore arise and take my place of prominence. (2) Whoever is occupying my sit of prominence, I dethrone you by fire in Jesus name.

You cannot be where they kept you again. When they come to look for you there, they shall hear this declaration about you: *"he is not here, for he has risen...* Matt.28: 6". They have no right to keep you there. If the Roman soldiers could not stop Jesus from rising, by resurrection power you shall rise to your next level in prominence. Shout fire!

Slaves Riding on Horseback

John 8: 34 tell us that every sinner is a slave; and God is saying that it is evil and an error for slaves to ride on horsebacks as princes. These people are driving the best cars, living in the best houses, manning the best offices and commanding great wealth at your expense. Proverbs 19: 10 say **"it is not right for slaves to rule over princes"**. How long shall this error continue? How long will the heathen continue to decide what is allotted to you? It is not God's will for slaves to decide your portion. Something supernatural must happen because until they are compelled to come down from your horse, you will continue trekking.

Prayer Point :(1) every slave riding on my horse and enjoying my appointed wealth, fall in the name of Jesus. (2) Whoever is sitting on my throne through demonic sacrifice, by the sacrifice of Jesus I dethrone you.

Princes Walking on Foot as Slaves

The devil is a liar; the table must turn for your favor. Revelation 1: 6 and 5: 10 reveal that we are kings and priests. When kings or princes begin to eat crumbs then you know something is terribly wrong. The crumbs belong to dogs. You were not created for crumbs or left overs. You are appointed for the meat on the table. You must continuously remember that you are the son of the king of the universe. Your days of trekking and sweating are over in the name of Jesus.

Prayer Point: (1) by the reason of the anointing, I break the yoke of enslavement in the name of Jesus (2) whoever is taking advantage of my trekking to ride and drive expire in Jesus name (3) whatever sacrifice was use to buy my place of honor, expire in the Jesus name (4) every slave riding my horse, come down let me climb

You must remember that the error came from the devil. He is the brain behind poverty among Christians. He wants to make your life miserable and uncomfortable. Satan's focus is to remove your attention from Christ and he is out to employ every avenue to do that; that includes making you poor.

Prayer Point: You devil in my world, you are an alien and a liar and cannot decide my destiny, fall like lightening in the name of Jesus.

Reasons for the Error

These reasons contribute to the error prevailing in the world. They include

Sin:

Ecclesiastes 10: 8 says whoever breaks through a wall will be bitten by a serpent. As long as the hedge of divine protection is not removed through sin, the serpent will not be able to strike. Sin is the reason many Christians are languishing in poverty. The bible rightly says that sin is a reproach to every people; and that he that covers his sin shall not prosper. It is righteousness that brings establishment. Righteousness will exalt you but sin brings reproach and downfall. So until you address the issue of sin, you are still at the mercy of the devil and he will continue to enforce the error revealed in Ecclesiastes 10: 5-7. But it is too late for the devil because the voice of the blood of Jesus is speaking on your behalf. Hallelujah.

Your desire:

But there was a certain beggar named Lazarus, full of sores, who was laid at his gate DESIRING to be fed with the crumbs which fell from the rich man's table...Luke 16: 21-21

The desire of most Christians is the reason for the poverty they suffer. Like Lazarus, many Christians are contented with the crumbs. Lazarus desired the crumbs that fell from the rich man's (a slave to sin) table. His desire demoted him to the class of dogs. The dogs in their aspiration for better meals left the crumbs for him and found his wounds more palatable. He died living on crumbs. Lazarus belonged to the old covenant but you belong to the new and superior covenant. Hence it is an abuse to the law of grace to live on crumbs. It is an insult to your person, having been born again to live from hand to mouth. You are not born again to suffer again. Step up on your desire because it fuels your expectation and your expectation facilitates your provision. **Until you expect, you cannot collect**. It is time to desire political offices and other honorable positions in life. Occupy them and release the righteousness of God until Christ comes.

Your Mindset:

Your location in life is a function of what occupies your mind. Your mentality is the reason for your locality. You are what you think. If you think rich, you grow to become rich but when you have a poverty stricken mentality, you will without doubt be poor. Your view about the subject of prosperity tells to a great extent if you will be rich or poor. The sinners who are occupying seats of power are people who think dominion. But you are the right person to think that way. Read more about mindset in subsequent chapters.

Scanty or no Prayers:

The people who control the spiritual and physical climate of an environment are those who prevail in prayers. To be weak in prayers is to be weak in power and void of dominion. Those who do not pray, end up liabilities in the kingdom. Jesus said men ought always to pray and not faint. **If you faint in prayer, the picture of your future will be faint.** Through prevailing prayers you can stop evil men, sack ungodly rulers and install a ruler after God's heart. Elijah by the voice of prophesies sacked king Ahazariah from the throne. And the Bible says this about him

Elijah was a man with a nature like ours, and he prayed earnestly... James 5: 17

The Christendom can decide what happens in our polity. It is time for the Christendom to sponsor righteous people to take up government position so as to enforce the kingdom lifestyle in our polity. We cannot continue speaking from the background where our ideas are treated with disdain. **It is time to complaint less, pray more and act timely**. Let us jointly release words to heaven so that the king of Glory will intervene in our polity. But as long as Christians leave their praying position and begin to complaint, the wicked will continue having a field day. Heaven is set to confirm our words.

Sacrifice:

The earth as long as it remains will continue to respond to seeds (sacrifices) through harvest. The earth is a precious jewel that goes to the highest bidder. The quantity and quality of sacrifice you make on earth determines the level of response you get. It is a petty however that the children of disobedience sacrifice more in various ways than Christians in recent times. This is why they are occupying enviable positions at the expense of Christians. God responds to sacrifice. The devil also responds to sacrifices. Your sacrifice will move you to move God. The wicked have learnt to give dangerously and this they have discovered from the Bible. This is why sinners are gradually taking charge of the earth. This was one of the errors that Jesus came to correct. He also showed us the way of sacrifice to go up. When Christ striped the devil of power and dominion, it included the right to a comfortable life. That was why the Comforter (the Holy

Spirit) came. He came to make us comfortable. Use the key of sacrifice.

Men of sacrifice are covenant people (Genesis 15; Psalm 50: 5). Sacrifice yourself, time, resources and whatever you possess in the service of God. This principle shall be revisited in subsequent chapters.

How to turn the Tables for Your Favor

Get Angry Mark 11: 11-17, 20. Anger is not bad when properly channeled.

Until you get angry at certain misnomer in your life, the devil won't let you be. When Jesus went to the fig tree when he was hungry, to get some fig fruit but had nothing to eat, He cursed the fig tree and it died within twenty four hours. There is power in your mouth. The power to kill and make alive is only activated when you open your mouth to speak insightfully. Silence is not always the best answer. Silence isn't a sign of humility but humiliation; it's not a sign of spirituality but stupidity. We are in a word warfare, so heaven only confirms what you say. Heaven will do nothing against what you permit. If you are angry with your present circumstance, arise as you begin to declare and do the word.

Fight Revelation 12: 7-11; Nehemiah 4: 14. You don't win, until you fight. We live-in an era where the violent take it by force. Things are naturally in a place of rest until force is applied. To be idle, lazy and leis-affaire will make your life a dumping ground. No fly dares a well heated iron. No spectator ever wins a price except he is diligently involved in the competition. No nominal Christian will win if he is not battle ready. God told Israelites that he had given them the land of Canaan to posses, but after this glorious declaration, He asked them to pick their weapons and fight. You fight to gain possession of your inheritance. Life is battle. To face life with folded arms is to invite untold hardship. You must remember that your table is prepared for you in the presence of your enemies (Psalm 23: 5). Nehemiah said, with one hand they built the house of God and with the other, armed themselves for battle against any enemy that attempt to stop them. **To be casual in life is to become a casualty.** If you don't want to end up a slave, arise and fight.

Bountiful Sacrifice Genesis 22: 1. Abraham earned a spot in the heart of

God and provoked the release of supernatural prosperity through dangerous sacrifice (the sacrifice of Isaac). Sacrifice provokes abundant harvest. God wanted a family and so He sacrificed Christ. The son of God then became the son of man so that sons of men will become sons of God. In this earth, harvest is a function of seeds. To live a seedless life is to apply for a stressful life. Satan learnt this principle from the word and has taught his agents and followers the corrupted version and the world is responding. You have the real thing. Sacrifice your way into a life of abundance. A young man called me in the middle of the night complaining how a contract of supplies he had was mysteriously taken from him and given to another. As I began to pray about it, the Lord whispered to me that the contract was stolen from him through a demonic sacrifice made. The earth you must know is a precious jewel that goes to the highest bidder. God swore not to destroy the world with flood ever again after Noah extinct some animals in the bid to sacrifice to God. Your sacrifice can change the cause of your generation for good. You can end the battles of your life through sacrifice. People have been miraculously healed because of sacrifice. Try it and you'll see that it works.

Secure Kingdom Power 2Kings 1: 9-15: The story of Elijah is insightful.

When the first and second army of fifties and their captains tried compelling Elijah to come down from a height, he commanded fire to fall and consume them and it happened promptly. There are many enemies fighting tirelessly to pull you down. But take your place of power and authority and refuse to go down. Whoever is fighting to pull you down, fire will settle the matter. The wicked at the apex can kill to maintain their positions. Most of them wipe out those they see as threat to their throne. According to Dr. Paul Enenche, **"power is needed for the overcoming of resistance, to facilitate progress in life, fulfill destiny, establish authority, silence the opposition, activate potentials and deliver the oppressed"**. It's divine power that puts you in control. Who is fighting to bring you down to the dust? Let fire come down for you to go up in the name of Jesus the Christ.

CHAPTER SEVEN

STOP THEM OR THEY WILL STOP YOU

...Moreover the dogs came and licked his sores... Luke 16: 21

The sores here stand for severe weakness. The amplified version tells us that Lazarus was carelessly dropped at the rich man's gate. We also see that instead of his weakness to attract helpers, it rather attracted dogs. Every dog occupying the place of your helpers will die in the mighty name of Jesus. The easiest way to gain dominion over your opponent is to discover his weakness. Victory is guaranteed when you exercise control through that weakness. Lazarus sores were not hidden from the dogs so they fearlessly came and feast fat from it. You can only be conquered when your weakness is known. Samson was conquered by the Philistines when Delilah helped them to uncover his point of weakness. As a Nazarite, he was to stay away from sexual immorality, strong drinks and cutting of his hair. When he violated these, the enemy defeated him. The enemy is interested in knowing your point of weakness; don't let him. When the dogs discovered Lazarus sores they concentrated on it, feasted and got fat and the more they did this, the weaker he became. **Lazarus' pain was the source of pleasure to the dogs**. It continued until they ate him to death. Arise and stop these dogs before they kill you untimely.

The wicked have discovered our weakness and are digging deep and opening it up the more as they feast fat and release severe pain on us. We are not Lazarus. Something must be done about this. We won't die and leave the dogs to stay alive to continue perpetuating this wickedness. It is defeat for you to die before dogs. The bible says we should beware of dogs; but it is time for them to also say beware of lions. You are a lion; no dog should defeat you. Judgment will not delay to fall on any demonic agent that wishes you death in Jesus name.

Prayer Point: I am not Lazarus, therefore any agent of darkness wishing me death, I return the arrow. **2.** I remove the teeth of every demonic dog; eat no more. **3.** Vampires! Leave me alone; eat your flesh and drink your blood in the name of Jesus. **4.** I refuse untimely death; therefore evil dogs die the death in the name of Jesus.

CHAPTER EIGHT

DESTROYING ATTACKERS OF SEEDS

And when the fowls came down upon the carcasses, Abram drove them away Genesis 15: 11

Your seed today contains your future harvest. To be void of seed is to be emptied of tomorrow. The enemy is interested in eating up what you sow as seen in the passage above. Only fools eat up their seeds during harvest. The first thing a farmer does during harvest is to select healthy yam seedlings for the next farming season. The seed you eat today will deprive you of harvest tomorrow. It applies more in the kingdom. God never allows a dedicated sower to stay without seed.

...That it may give seed to the sower and bread to the eater Isaiah 55: 10

While God commits to giving seed to sowers, the devil is in the business of attacking the seed of sowers. He knows too well that sowers in the kingdom are threat to his kingdom, since they have conquered greed through their much giving. He thus, concentrates on attacking their seeds. Matthew 13 verses 24 and 25 are instructive:

... The kingdom of heaven is like a man who sowed good seed in his field: but while men slept, his enemy came and sowed tares among the wheat and went his way.

So you see, there is an enemy that does not want you to prosper. He is bent at making your seeds dead or weakening them to cause unhealthy and premature harvest. This is the reason many committed givers, sow without tangible evidence of bountiful harvest. It is written that when you give it shall be given back to you in good measure, pressed down, shaking together and running over. And you know what? The scripture cannot be broken. Those the devil cannot corrupt with stinginess, he attacks their seeds just to get at their harvest. You need to know your enemy to be able to destroy him. Time has come to destroy all those attacking your seeds. They attack your seed to get at your harvest and you know whatever targets your harvest is after your joyful future. There is life in every seed. Whatever tempers with your seed is after your life. So it is time to react against attackers of your seeds. The following enemies are after the seeds you sow:

Devourers:

... Behold, a sower went out to sow and as he sowed, some seed fell by the wayside; and the BIRDS came and DEVOURED them Matthew 13: 3,4

There are enemies whose sole responsibility is to devour your seed to keep you in perpetual want. These enemies watch you as you plant your financial seeds on various grounds and then go for the seeds to devour them. This is why your tithes and offerings must be in place to provoke a supernatural rebuke on devourers around you.

And I will rebuke the devourer for your sakes, so he will not destroy the fruit of your ground, nor shall the vine fail to bear fruit for you in the field, says the Lord of hosts Malachi 3: 11

In Matthew 13 verse 4 says "and the birds came and devoured them"; in Amos 4 verse 9, it is said that "the locust devoured them". The devourers of your seeds are waiting at the slightest opportunity to attack your seeds but I challenge you to arise and execute on them the written judgment. This is your honor as a saint.

To execute on them the written judgment, this honor has all His saints Psalm 149: 9

Chokers of Seeds:

And some fell among thorns, and the thorns sprang up and choked them Matthew 13: 7

The word choke means to prevent from breathing by constricting or obstructing the throat or depriving of air. It also means to fill (a space) so as to make movement difficult or impossible. The passage above says that "the thorns sprang up and choked them (the seed)". To spring means to move suddenly or rapidly upwards or forwards. To spring up means to suddenly develop or appear. There are enemies that appear all of a sudden just to attack your planted seeds. Notice that both the devourers and chokers of seeds don't attack the seed in your hand because they know there is no future for such seeds. They are after your planted seeds to mess up your future. When chokers of seeds appear, they deprive your seed of air, nutrients and the freedom to move, grow, mature and bear fruits. Arise and exercise your authority as a son of the kingdom by destroying these enemies.

Corrupters of seeds:

The kingdom of heaven is like a man who sowed good seed in his field; but while men slept, his enemy came and sowed tares among the wheat and went his way Matthew 13:24, 25

Jesus here was using an earthly issue to talk about the kingdom of heaven. He noted that a man sowed good seed in his field. But in the process of time an enemy came in when men were asleep to sow tares among the wheat and went his way. Tares are harmful weeds resembling corn when young. The enemy capitalized on the weakness of men to sow the harmful weeds just to attack the planted seed. No wonder the bible admonish us to watch and pray. To sow your seeds and go to bed without watering them with your prayers gives the enemy unhindered access to attack your seed. There is every need to pray fervently as we anticipate bountiful harvest.

Factors in Seed Sowing

There are four factors in seed sowing necessary for the kind of harvest one gets. They include God, the sower, the seed and the soil. God is the sole creator and owner of the other factors. He gives the sower the intellect, skill, strength and the general know how to select and plow his soil and plant the kind, quality and quantity of seed. The mind of the sower that helps him understand when, where and how to sow what, is a gift from God. While man sows and sometime waters the seed, it is God that gives the increase.

However, as a matter of principle, seeds only thrive in fertile soils. It therefore means that the sower plants his seed on soils that will support his seed. No wise sower plants on infertile grounds. No matter how good the seed is, if it is planted on the wrong soil, it won't produce the anticipated result. The best ground to plant your seed is in evangelism. Others include giving to meet church needs, giving to your man of God, parents, wife and children and the needy.

PART THREE

TRANSITION ZONE

CHAPTER NINE

THE POWER OF WHAT YOU KNOW

Your worst enemy is not the devil but ignorance. The devil cannot destroy you. If he could, he would have done it before now. Backwardness is the result of ignorance. The status you attain in life is a function of the level of knowledge you access.

My people are destroyed for lack of knowledge... Hosea 4:6

In life, to be in control or under control, a master or the slave is a function of what you know. Your freedom is proportionate to the amount of truth you know. The short cut to destroying the power of ignorance is access to revelation.

And you shall know the truth and the truth shall make you free John 8:32

No amount of prayer and fasting can break the yoke of poverty off a person if he does not make conscious effort to obey scriptural principles for prosperity. It is the principles of God (His expertise) that culminates into prosperity. Your sacrifices of fasting and prayers cannot knock the simple principle of obeying the laws governing prosperity.

... Behold, to obey is better than sacrifice, and to heed than the fat of rams 1Samuel 15:22

If you are willing and obedient, you shall eat the good of the land Isaiah 1:19

So you see that your lengthy prayers and fasting cannot alter divine laws of prosperity. But your prayers become effective when they are backed by obedience to these laws. God honors His word very highly. Hence anyone who lives by the word, obtain the blessings it carries. As you read the Bible- a book written by the most successful individual alive- God, you will discover two things about Him- His person and His principles. Knowing His person brings you holiness and prepares you for heaven but His principles prepares you for a successful life on earth. To know His person but His principles only makes you heaven bound but stranded in the earthly realm. The story of Lazarus is instructive. Also to know God's principles and not know His person only brings success to you on earth but grants you no access to heaven (Hebrews 12:14). You however need a balanced encounter with the person and principles of God to be heaven bound and earthly useful.

What you know stirs boldness within you to stand before kings and giants. For David to challenge Goliath fearlessly, he knew what Saul and his army were ignorant of. Moses ran away from Pharaoh when he did not know enough about God, himself and what he had in his hand (the rod). His ignorance kept him in the wilderness, a place of stress, and became a servant to his father-in-law for years until he encountered God and gained access to revelation. It was only then, that he boldly stood before Pharaoh. Until you gain the right knowledge on prosperity, you remain in the wilderness of poverty. Insight makes you outstanding. You need understanding to be outstanding. To lack understanding is to remain under things you were created to rule over. You can only stand out when you are connected to earth shaking mysteries. What you know is what gives you the stamina to endure the present challenges. The Bible said about Jesus, "Who for the joy that was set before him, endured the cross". You must know to be known.

What then do you need to know to transit from poverty to prosperity? Read on.

CHAPTER TEN

MONEY

Money is a medium of exchange for goods and services. This means to possess wealth, there must be something in your hand to exchange. **If you have nothing to exchange, your condition will not change.** You will only be living at the mercy of people until you possess something in your hand to exchange. Money cannot come to you until it sees something tangible in your hand. You must possess what somebody else needs to be able to exchange it for their money. What goods do you have and what service can you render? This is how you migrate from poverty to prosperity. To be void of goods and services is to apply for poverty in its highest degree.

The amount of money you command is a simple function of the quality and quantity of goods you possess and the service you render. The price of lands can never be the same. A land loaded with resource will command more money than a land void of it. What do you have? God will bless you from what you have. For Elisha to prophesy prosperity on the late prophet's wife, he asked her what she had in her house. Inflow of money answers to the following:

- The quality and quantity of goods you have. A mud house and a concrete house with up to date facilities can never be on the same price list. People will pay any amount for quality. Inferior goods attract less income. Only the poor mentally and financially crave for quantity because it is inferior and cheap. Your ability to distribute your goods also increases the flow of money into your hands.
- The quality of service you deliver determines the patronage you command. You don't expect a seasoned fashion designer to be on

the same level of prosperity with a road side tailor who is only interested in cutting and sawing. The quality of service you deliver is a function of the training and skill you acquired. A seasoned architect will always be the boss of a bricklayer. Of course both of them will not command the same income. There is room for improvement in what ever you do. Until you improve on yourself, you won't meet up with current market demands.

- Accessibility of goods and services. The amount of money that flows into your hand is a function of how accessible your goods or services are to your market. Lands in towns and cities are sold for higher prices than lands in remote areas. Also the status of an individual or organization interested in what you have to offer determines the kind of money you receive. Make what you have readily available.
- The level of demand. The higher the demand on your goods or service delivery, the larger the inflow of income and vice versa.
- Your location. Where you market your goods or render services influences the level of income flow you command. A man who drives the president of a country will not be on the same pay schedule with a secondary school driver. The one that teaches in the university and the one in the secondary school are all teachers, but they are not earning the same salary.

All I am trying to portray is that you need something in your hand to attract good money from the pockets, wallets, bags and accounts of people.

Money is a measure of value. Just as kilometer is a measure for distance, kilogram for weight, seconds and minutes for time, so also money measures value. The level of prosperity you command is a function of the value you attain. How relevant are you to people? What is your level of significance? What is your level of contribution to people? **Recognition is a function of reasonable service**. Money flows towards these directions. You must strive to improve on yourself. If you are a road side tailor, undertake training as a fashion designer. You don't wish to lecture in the university with NCE or diploma simply because you have taught in the primary and secondary school for years. You need a strong first degree, a masters or a doctorate degree to qualify. You may say but God is a miracle God. Yes He is, but He is also a principled God. Peter said to the lamed man at the beautiful gate "such as I have, I give you". God won't commit to your hands what you cannot handle. In the parable of the talent, the master of the house gave his servants talents according to their abilities. You must also know that bribing your way into having degrees does not help, because your value is not just the certificate but the level of knowledge you have acquired. As a Pastor, improve on your preaching and bible studies. Get ministry materials and study to become a blessing to your pew. If you are not blessing them, you are wasting their precious time. They won't come back to you; talk more of blessing you with their resources. Make yourself significantly relevant to people and money will flow into your hands.

Money is also known as currency. This means money is meant to flow. You need to create a means for money to flow to handle tangible wealth. Create a circle for the money that leaves your hand to come back, which is only how you can command wealth. When you cut the circle of money flow, it simply means, that which leaves your hand will rarely come back to you. This can expose you to lack. Make a fence for the money in your hand to multiply continuously.

You must know that money is good. You need it to gain certain levels of comfort. Money is not the root of evil as many say referring to the bible. The bible didn't say that. It is the love of money that is the foundation of every evil. When you are in control of money, it is good, but when the love of money is in control of you, it is dangerous. The love of money is the reason for most occult practices such as ritualism, robbery, 419, and embezzlement. The love of money has turned many into heartless, brutal beasts. How do you explain it for a man to pound a life baby, behead people and sacrifice loved ones? There is a better alternative in the scriptures.

Money is a reward for solving a problem. Money represents power, influence, achievement and security. That is why money is deceptive. Jesus referred to this as "deceitfulness of riches" which arrests spiritual development (Matthew 13:22). It is a false sense of security. Money can provide security gargets but life; it can give you a house but a home; it can give you a woman but a wife; it can give you power and influence but certainly not against the devil. Money can give you mansions here on earth but heavens, except you are born again. You need to know this so you don't give yourself to bondage. Money should not take the place of God in your life. It is dangerous.

Money does not change you. It simply makes more of whatever you really are. Money is an amplifier; it reveals your nature. If you are a proud man, when money comes it amplifies your pride. Money amplifies your true nature. One of the greatest needs of life is money. The reason for unfulfillment and frustration among thousands is because they are ignorant of the truth about money. The abuse and misuse of money can be very destructive. Money will affect you (Proverbs 27:24; 23:5) but control it with the word of God.

Money is a tool. While money may become a snare to the unbelievers, it is the Christians' tool for effective evangelization. Money in the hand of Christians is a threat to the devil and his kingdom.

Why the Rich are different from the Poor

1. the poor eat their seed (capital) but the rich sow and invest theirs
2. The poor and middle class want to live like the rich, so they buy luxuries. The rich don't spend that way; they multiply their money and live off the overflow
3. the rich know how to identify opportunities, whereas the poor do not see opportunities
4. the rich have the "can do" mindset, but the poor rely on miracles or luck Proverbs 10: 4
5. poverty is not a state of the purse or pocket, but a state of the mind
6. for the majority of time, the poor are not doing enough in efficient manner, but the rich are experts at what they do and are diligent in their work
7. poverty come because of lack of management but the rich know how to manage resources
8. poverty is lack of savings and investment but the rich understand and practice savings and investment

9 the poor have not learnt how to reduce their expenses, but the rich have learnt to overcome their appetite
10 the poor are afraid of failing but the rich take risks
11 the poor work for money but money works for the rich
12 the rich go for assets before liabilities but the poor follow after liabilities so they can look like the rich
13 The rich engage their minds from the beginning of a job to the end before using their hands but the poor work more with their hands than their minds.
14 The rich and poor have equal time (24 hours), but what differentiates them is how they use the time at their disposal.

Nuggets for financial success

- Financial success begins when you understand the difference between assets and liabilities, investment mentality and a consumer mentality as well as financial discipline and instant gratification
- build a career that can carry you; a career that has great future
- Creating multi-streams of income makes you more prosperous than owning a source of income.
- There is a great difference between owning a business and being self employed. A business that needs your presence always to function is not a business; you are just self-employed. A business functions with or without your presence.
- Create yearly, monthly or daily targets. It will motivate you to plan and have focus. It controls your spending on casual wishes and provokes your attention towards your priorities.
- God gives us authority, intellect, wisdom and ideas, in other words, the abilities to make money ourselves Deut. 8: 18
- God blesses a diligent worker rather than an idle person who is just hoping for blessings to fall from heaven on him
- If you want to be rich and wealthy, get involved in the production of goods and services. Money is a reward for goods and services; it is a compensation for going through the process of production
- Money is a good servant but a bad master. Command rule over it and not the other way round
- Money should not determine what you can and cannot afford

- Lack of money limits one's desire and visions. It dictates their lifestyle and controls their actions. It tells them what they can eat, what they can wear, where they live and where they go.
- Wealth is not a miracle; it must be either earned or created. Make your choice
- Wealth and riches are not about how much you make but how much you keep
- Money is just a means, not an end; it is a means for solving certain problems and not all problems because money also fails Genesis 47: 15
- If money does not serve the kingdom, then it perverts, spoils and destroys its owners
- Money is neutral; it is an amplifier; it also enslaves
- It is wisdom to understand that the first talent or money that comes to us is not for spending. Sow it into good soil, which is the beginning of producing fruit or profit. This is the difference between the rich and the poor
- The rich make profit from their money and the poor consume theirs quickly, afraid someone will take it from them
- You must make conscious efforts to discipline yourself to control the lust and desire to spend money
- Discipline yourself to balance your expenses with income. Never allow your expenses go above your income. Ensure you have reserve from your income
- When you put your seed to work, it multiplies. By disuse, it depreciates and loses value. Storing money away without putting it to work will lose its original value over time especially in third world countries where inflation is the order of the day
- Money will always leave the hands of those who don't put it to use and come to the hands of those willing to multiply it. Learn from the parable of the talent in Matthew 25: 14-30
- The key to increase is always investment. A good steward keeps what he or she receives, then uses and increases it through investments. Those who invest their talent are entrusted with more
- The reward for being trustworthy is more trust; the steward who buries his sum, loses what he has and he will see it given to another

- Every Christian who desires to save for investment must begin by paying God first. You must make the paying of your tithes and offerings an automatic practice. After God, pay yourself by keeping a proportion of your income as your savings. Make it a consistent practice.
- Reduce non essential expenditures. Learn to live according to your purse. Don't spend money on things you can do without; they are unnecessary but they rob you of good money over time. This is the paradox of money; people spending more than they earn Eccl. 5: 11
- Don't be in a hurry to invest. Take great caution so that you do not lose your money. Seek counsel and know more about an opportunity before investing
- Develop a budget and live by it. A budget defends your priorities from casual wishes and it helps you to differentiate between the two
- Beware of lending out money. You are not a bank, so do not bring others burdens on yourself. It is not selfishness but a guiding principle to growing your finances
- Money comes to those who are already rich in knowledge of laws of money. If you are not already rich in your mind, then money won't come to you
- Understand the laws of money which are multiplication, retention and diligence. This is the way to wealth.
- Rich countries are rich because they supply things that are scarce but in high demand. Poor countries are poor because they supply too many things for which there is relatively little demand
- The giving law is only one of many laws of prosperity; by itself it will fail to make anyone sustainably wealthy
- The main purpose of money is not to meet needs, but first to accomplish God's purposes on the earth, which is evangelization.
- You are made rich to reach out to others. God is more interested in making us channels of blessing to others rather than islands of blessing to ourselves Gen. 12: 2-3
- It is wickedness to desire what you haven't worked for Prov. 12: 12 (NIV). Success comes through hard work.

- Successful people know that success isn't a gamble or a matter of chance. **A lucky man isn't a successful man**. Give a fool a million dollar and in the next few months, he will be broke again.
- Real success is a lifetime of learning. You succeed by learning continuously. Successful people learn from others and from their failures and success.

CHAPTER ELEVEN

SECRETS OF THE PROSPEROUS

What secrets of the prosperous do you know?

Thus says the LORD; "stand in the ways and see, and ask for the old paths, where the good way is, and walk in it; then you will find rest for your soul... Jeremiah 6:16

I have witness Christians pray and fast to be prosperous, sow seeds, claim prophesies with offerings but when you ask them how many books they have read on financial success and secrets of prosperous people, they tell you none. How then do you secure secrets to prosper? The text above reveals you stand in their ways to observe, ask questions, find out their secrets and walk in it, and then your rest will manifest.

"...labor therefore to enter into that rest." Hebrews 4:11

Whatever you desire to become in life, there is someone already excelling in it. **Behind their glory, is a story. Ask for the story and you will access your glory**. What you know about them will add up to what you already know. Their challenges will give you a clue of what to expect and how to overcome it. Their success story will motivate you and push you into success. Success is not a function of chance but of choice. You don't gamble to be great; you plan and make frantic efforts. You work it out. Success is progressive. The speed you command is a function of laid down plans and your motivation. You are not expected to jump; those who do, fall by gravity because they lack the foundation to sustain them. Only those who grow into success abide. A million pounds in the hands of a fool is useless because in less than no time he will waste it in prodigality.

God won't give you what you cannot manage effectively. It is your right to be blessed as a citizen of the kingdom but until you are ready to manage wealth, God does not release it. What you learn about successful people will place you in a ready position to get and manage wealth. Learn from their discipline, diligence, devotion, dedication, commitment as well as their managerial principles. This is the way you gain command of the true riches of God.

When you study the success habits of great achievers, you will notice an obvious and outstanding quality; **they are very conscious of time**. They consistently walk and work with time. They don't give room for what Nigerians call African time, where you schedule a meeting for 8.00am but begin at 8.30am. A church should be committed to time, when she begins her service and when the service should end, if she must command success. It applies to every sector of life.

A close look at the genuinely prosperous will reveal time as their life's precious commodity. It is the currency of time that helps them strengthen their families, birth ideas, and achieve their dreams and goals. Your respect for time will ignite the ability for its effective management. Learn the rich man's approach to time and you will move into their league. If you must know; **the rich and the poor have the same hours in a day at their disposal; the difference between them is what each does with his own time**. Make your choice now. Mike Murdock posited that **champions make decisions that create the future they desire and losers make decisions that create the present they desire**. Don't act like Esau who in the bid to satisfy the present mortgaged his glorious future. He sought for it with tears but couldn't get it back. He loosed his place in the patriarchal family.

Successful people have cultivated a total focus on their assignment. This is very important for success in life. Mark a minister who is focused on his assignment, he will come out very successful. It applies to anyone. The time you invest in a thing unveils your passion for it. **You will only succeed with something that is an obsession**.

...but this one thing I do, forgetting those things which are behind and reaching forth unto those things which are before, I press toward the mark for the prize of the higher calling of God in Christ Jesus Philippians 3: 13-14

Successful people read continuously, listen attentively and also ask questions that help them advance toward their assignment. They are committed to hunting opportunities and turning them into their desired miracles. You must develop a reading and studying habit. You are only approved when you study. Your studying will qualify you for a show (2 Timothy 2: 15). Abraham Lincoln once said **I will study; I will prepare myself, because some day, my time will come.** You must be a good listener and learn from what you hear. According to Mike Murdock, **listen to happy people for encouragement; listen to unhappy voices for ideas.** Don't just listen; ask questions for clarity of information. Don't ask the one you are listening to, questions outside his area of experience or specialization. You may not get the facts you seek. Seek for the right people.

Uncommon Achievers disconnect from people who do not appreciate their time. Apostle Johnson Suleman once said **a bad friend is like a flat tire; you don't change it, you don't go anywhere.** If you value someone, you will appreciate his time. You need people around you who talk to the king in you, not those who expose the kid in you. Avoid people who continuously subtract from you and add no value to you. As a matter of principle successful people never go to places where they are tolerated but are consistently found where they are celebrated. Your better can only become best where you are celebrated. You must know and master the environment you find yourself. This is because your environment contributes to whether you end up a success or a failure. Note; **until Satan attacks your atmosphere, he cannot conduct your destiny (Johnson Suleman).**

CHAPTER TWELVE

SUCCESS

What do you know about success? The will of God for you is prosperity, good success, a future and a hope.

Beloved, I pray that you may prosper in all things and be in health just as your soul prospers 3John 2

... That you may observe to do according to all that is written. For then you will make your way prosperous, and then you will have good success Joshua 1:8

For I know the thoughts that I think toward you, says the LORD, thoughts of peace and not evil, to give you a future and a hope Jeremiah 29:11

What do you see when you think of success? What you become in life is a function of:

- o What you hear
- o What you think (your mind set)
- o What you see (your vision) and
- o What you do (your activities)

Hearing and Listening

What you continuously hear and listen to produces the faith you need to become or the fear that makes you unable to become. So you need to screen thoroughly what you hear and listen to because it forms the bases of what you begin to think and do.

So then faith comes by hearing and hearing by the word of God **Romans 10:17**

The faith you receive from hearing and listening to the word of God stimulates incredible favor from God and His angels. Now hearing and listening have slight difference. That is the reason I am using them together. Hearing speaks of the ability to perceive (a sound) with the ear while listening is the ability to give one's attention to a sound. While the later requires concentration, the former is passive. Hearing tells you the song is playing but listening tells you what the song is all about. What you hear or listen to can either inform, reform and transform your life or inform and deform your destiny. It therefore behooves on us to give ourselves to Biblical information that guarantees transformation.

The law of the LORD is perfect, converting the soul (the mind); the testimony of the LORD is sure, making wise the simple. The status of the LORD is right, rejoicing the heart; the commandment of the LORD is pure, enlightening the eyes **Psalm 19:7-8**

When the word of God gains entrance into you, it renews your mind and brings total transformation to your person.

And He said to them, be careful what you are hearing. The measure [of thought and study] you give [to the truth you hear] will be the measure [of virtue and knowledge] that comes back to you—and more [besides] will be given to you {who hear} Mark 4:24 (amp.)

Thinking

This speaks of your imaginative power. It is the picture you paint in your mind that is plotted for you. Your picture is your future. What you picture is the future you capture. What you become is traced to what occupied your mind. You are what you think. In life, you either think or stink. If you don't think, you'll sink. Your locality is a function of your mentality. Your functionality, creativity, productivity are all tied to your mentality. The authority you command and your audacity in life answer to your mentality. Your mindset will either set things in order or bring disorder to your life. Your mindset creates your complex. What are you thinking? What is always on your mind about yourself? What is continuously there can create a future for you. Your mind paints the picture of your future.

According to Mike Murdock, your mind is divided into two parts namely, your memory and your imagination. Your memory replays your past while your imagination preplays the future. It is the key to your future. The following is instructive

- You will always move in the direction of your strongest and most dominant thought.
- Your imagination is an invisible machine inside your mind that creates pictures of something in your future. Pictures of those things you desire. One of the most beautiful gifts God has given you is your mind. One is your memory; the other is your imagination. Both are God-given gifts that can make or mar you. Your memory will photograph, file and replay pictures of your past. Your imagination on the other hand, creates and preplay things you want to happen in your future.
- Great achievers have learned to replay the memories of their past triumph and preplay the pictures of their desired successes. The story of David and Goliath is instructive.
- Miracles begin in the soil of your imagination. God plants dream within you. Then, that dream is incubated in the room of your imagination. Genesis 3:16; 26:4.
- Your imagination strengthens your faith in God
- Imagination compels result Genesis 11:6
- Your imagination can unleash unprecedented energy.
- Jesus used His imagination to picture the future rewards of His suffering.
- Your imagination is a motivator and a stimulator to doing incredible things in life.
- Your imagination controls you Philippians 4:8
- It is your responsibility to control your mind and imagination. Thoughts will invade your imagination from everywhere; thoughts of fear and unbelieve (what Mike Murdock calls disaster seeds) planted by Satan as well as thoughts of miracles and blessings (what he calls dream seeds) planted by God all enters your mind. Your imagination is not a referee. It will not judge whether the seeds

going into your mind are good or bad. It will simply grow whatever seeds you decide to water and nurture. This is one of the reasons we need the Holy Spirit and the word of God in our lives. The Holy Spirit will help you harness and focus your imagination to grow your dream.

- o You can change what has been happening in your life by focusing your imagination. You can reverse yesterday's wrong decision by making a good decision today.
- o Refuse to misuse your imagination Romans 1:21
- o Your imagination can move you from the pit to the palace. The story of Joseph is instructive.

I charge you to use your mind. Don't just work; reason things out before you use your hands. A job concluded in the mind reduces stress in the hand. The reason for labor and little result is because the mind is not fully utilized. Even God ask that we come and reason with Him (Isaiah 1:18). Those who use their minds command control over those who only use their hands. Jacob rose from the position of a house boy in his father-in-law's house to a commander of wealth when he engaged his mind (Genesis 30:37-43). Use your mind. It is your servant and not your boss. If you desire to be a high flyer, engage your imagination.

What you see

This is the same as vision. The reason for much television is Christendom today is because most Christians are so lazy to access visions. Satan desires to replace your vision with television. What you keep seeing creates a picture of what you become. Until you are able to see it with your mind's eye, your hand can't handle it. You can only receive grace to cease what you see. Heaven is only committed to give you what you are able to see. The extent of your vision determines the extent of your possession.

... Lift your eyes now and look from the place where you are...for all the land which you see, I give to you and your descendants forever Genesis 13:14-15

So what God gives you is a function of what you are able to see. What you are able to see in the word of God is what God is committed to perform in your life (Jeremiah 1:11-12). What you keep seeing determines your focus

(Psalm 101:3). What God will author and finish in your life is a function of who you are looking on. Don't claim to be looking on God when your hope is on a man somewhere. Where you steadfastly look on determine the direction from where your help comes from (Psalm 121).

God is interested in your vision and wants to deliver it to you. The devil is afraid of your vision and wants to destroy that ability. That accounted for why Samson loosed his eyes to the Philistines when Delilah caused him to lose his strength. A lost vision begets a lost future. **Life becomes a fiction without vision**. To live without a vision is to be friend frustration. Where are you seeing yourself five years from now? Vision creates concentration as well as a planned and disciplined life. Vision is the warehouse of success. Where you are today is a function of yesterday's vision. I dare to tell you to dream big because your God is big. Great visions create great destinies. Have a vision and heaven will confirm it. Your age and location isn't an excuse. If you can conceive that dream, heaven will release grace for its achievement.

What you do

Things don't just happen; people make them happen. Don't sit there wishing; do something. After your faith talk and seed faith, don't just sit and fold your hands for money to begin to fall from heaven, lay your hands on a work. That is where God commits Himself to blessing you.

...That you may observe to do according to all that is written in it Joshua 1:8.

Every successful man is found doing something. Don't just do something but do something reasonable. If you are building a career let it be one that brings great future. You must understand that what you do consistently creates a habit; your habit creates your future. Your miracles come in doing. Faith talk minus handwork equals poverty. Your complaint will only worsen your situation; do something. Peter will only have a great catch of fish when he stops complaining and analyzing his situation, and then venture into the deep to lay down his net. Uncommon people do daily what common people do occasionally. Everything you are doing today is becoming a habit and your habit is creating your destiny. The quality of time you spend doing a particular thing reveals your passion for it. Channel your energy to doing things that will create a better future for you. Also plan what you do for proper time management and effective result. Money increases in your hand when you begin to gain precision and accuracy on what you constantly do. Also keep a good relationship with people because you need them to succeed. The money you need is in their hands. One good relationship is capable of connecting you to four powerful and useful people to you. It also applies the other way round. Faith utterances without actions produce dead results. Even Jesus instructed that we should be doers of the word. Do something! Do something! Do something reasonable.

What is success?

Jesus has graciously given us the keys of the kingdom. You need the right key to open a given door. Keys are specially made tools for opening doors. In the kingdom, keys are principles or laws. It speaks of God's expertise. We don't prosper the world's way but God's way. God has standards. The existence of keys is a clear indication that there are doors to open. Each door has its key. The Bible is the master key since it houses all other keys. Prayer is not the key but a key in the kingdom. It is not enough to have a bunch of keys (the Bible); you need to know what key opens which door else you will still be stranded. Every great door is opened by a small key. You won't need to exert energy when you have the small key in your hand. A keyless door is a useless door.

Everyone has three days- yesterday (your past), today (your present), and tomorrow (your future). **Your yesterday is in the tomb; your tomorrow is the womb**. Your memory replays your past but your imagination create and preplay your future. Where you are today is a function of how yesterday was handled. What you are doing now is creating a future for you. I charge you to put your hands on the plough and do the right thing for the palace you dream to possess. Your dream and work today must agree, to produce your desired future. Let me deal with what success is not before we see what success is.

What success not

Many have misunderstood success and prosperity and I shall make effort to correct it here by stating what success is not.

- o Success is not possession of good houses, cars, clothes and huge bank accounts. You can possess all these and still be unhappy and in secured. Money can buy you a good house but cannot buy you a home; money can build you a hospital but cannot buy you health. Our lovely late president Yar'adua died of a terminal disease and money couldn't stop it. Money will build a security outfit for you but cannot stop death from getting to you. Late president Abacha will tell you better. Money cannot buy life, so don't take life to get it. Money also fails people Genesis 47: 15-16. Have it God's way if you want peace of mind.

... The money failed in the land of Egypt and in the land of Canaan... Genesis 47:15

- o Success is not power, position, prestige and popularity. They don't bring peace of mind.
- o Success is not achieving self made goals. It does not guarantee genuine satisfaction. King Solomon, the wisest man that ever lived, with his entire splendor called all these vanity and vexation of the soul.

This is what the word says to a believer reading this life changing tool

... Do not worry. Saying, what shall we eat? Or what shall we drink? Or what shall we wear... For after all these things the Gentiles (unbelievers) seek... Matt. 6:31, 32

The Lord knows you need them and has provided the way to get these things and still have our peace which surpasses all understanding.

...For your heavenly Father knows that you need all these things. But seek first the kingdom of God and His righteousness, and all these things shall be added to you Matt. 6:32, 33

These things I have mentioned are not the basics of prosperity but additions. They are added to you to spice your life and enhance you the ability to fulfilling God's purpose.

What then is success?

In the kingdom, **success is to know and attain God's goals for your life**. Most People tend to run their lives based on the views of people about them. Their views about you most times negate God's purpose. When you fulfill their views at the expense of your God given purpose, you are not a success. This is one reason for unfulfilled purpose. Moses saw himself as nobody before Pharaoh; God called him a god over Pharaoh.

But Moses said to God, who am I that I should go to Pharaoh... Exo.3:11

So the Lord said to Moses: See, I have made you as God to Pharaoh... Exo.7: 1

Jeremiah had a wrong view of himself because of the crowd. He saw himself as a child but before his birth, he was ordained a prophet from the womb (Jeremiah 1: 5, 6); Jonah was comfortable to be a prophet in Tarshish but his call was to prophesy in Nineveh (Jonah1: 2, 3). Beloved of God, **to seek success outside God's will is to place yourself against a mighty tempest**. Those who run their lives by public opinion possess the grasshopper mentality. Follow after God and secure your purpose for living. In the words of Mike Murdock, success is

- **Becoming what God wants you to become**
- **Doing what God wants you to do**
- **Possessing what God wants you to own**

As you achieve the goals God has set for your life, then you become successful. Success you must note is progressive. It is a journey; it is movement. In the kingdom, jumping is not permitted. Those who jump fall by gravity but those who grow abide. The law of gravity is powerless when it meets a person who grew into prosperity. A jumper is at the mercy of the law of gravity.

Success means different things to different people depending on their position in God's maturity schedule (Mike Murdock, 2002). Every child of God has the right to succeed (John1: 12) but you need to be ready (matured) by the word to enjoy it. This is because

> *... The heir, as long as he is a child, does not differ at all from a slave, though he is the master of all, but is under guardians and stewards until the time appointed by the father Galatians 4: 1, 2*

The book in your hand is a tool graciously handed over to you to mature you and bring your appointed season of prosperity which is now. Mike Murdock once posited that **unbelievers often ignore the problems of prosperity while believers often ignore the purpose of prosperity. I find this true and revealing.**

Success also means different things to different people at different times. A young millionaire of about 40years will utterly be disappointed at a man of 85years who is celebrating his first one million dollar. The young man will look at the older fellow as a frustrated person. At age 85 the man is living by the grace of God. The chances here are that he may not live long to enjoy his wealth.

Prayer Point: Oh God! Visit me early in Jesus name.

It is having purpose in life, not possessions, that is truly satisfying and it can only be realized in Jesus (1John 5: 12). God has success plan for you spiritually, physically, emotionally, financially, socially and in your family. God has provided a golden key to help you unlock the doors of success on every side.

Golden keys to success

- Return to God Job 22:23-30; Mal.3:7
- Have a personal knowledge of God Exo.3: 6. 14
- Discover who you are in God Exo.3: 11; 7:1
- Discover those you are assigned to Exo.3: 10
- Understand your assignment Exo.4: 2-4
- Know the enemy you are anointed to defeat Exo.3:10
- Discover the rod (the gift) in your hand Exo.4:2
- Practice and exercise with the gift to gain perfection Exo.4: 2-4
- Exhibit God's grace before those you are assigned to Exo.4: 29-31
- Exercise dominion with the gift in your hand Exo.7: 10-12

To have a better understanding of the golden keys, order and read my book titled **"What Is That in Your Hand?"**

CHAPTER THIRTEEN

PLANNING

A plan is a detailed proposal for doing or achieving something. It is an intention or decision about what one is going to do. It is the map or diagram showing a layout of a given future you desire. Great men plan. It is the starting point for any dream or goal that you possess. You are only as successful as your plan. Life begins with planning. Even the all knowing God planned before creating man. If God did, then it is dangerous to live a plan less life.

For which of you, intending to build a tower, does not sit down first and count the cost, whether he has enough to finish it, lest after he has laid the foundation, and is not able to finish, all who see it begin to mock him, saying, this man began to build and was not able to finish Luke 14: 28-30.

A man that refuses to plan, signs application for frustration. Failing to plan is unconsciously planning to fail. When you are void of plans, you are robbed of glorious future. Progress requires a good sense of planning. Planning is as powerful as prayer. If you are not planning, you are playing with destiny. Wake up and plan your way into greatness. A plan is a written list of arranged actions necessary to achieve your desired goal.

... Write the vision; make it plain upon tables, that he may run that reads it Habakkuk 2: 2

The word 'write' is a command. But the command is not the plan. A command can take a moment but the plan can involve your lifetime. Men who plan are always honored by God. Noah planned the building of the Ark; Solomon planned the building of the great temple of God. God is a master planner. The Bible is His plan for mankind, the world and eternity.

Understand that as powerful as prayer is, it does not replace planning as planning also does not replace praying. Planners are always in control. The essence of planning is for progress, continuity, productivity, elimination of waste and accomplishment.

PROCESS OF PLANNING

Sit down first

For which of you, intending to build a tower, does not sit down first and count the cost, whether he has enough to finish it Luke 14:28

It is dangerous to act before thinking. You don't act before thinking. It works the other way round. You also don't need to pray more and plan less. You must balance praying and planning to give the desired future. Sit down to plan because your rising begins with sitting. **If you lack good base, you will be denied good height.** People mock at a man who starts but cannot complete his goal. Verses 29 and 30 of Luke 14 says **" *lest, after he has laid the foundation, and is not able to finish, all who see it begin to mock him, saying, this man began to build and was not able to finish*".**

You must learn to have a clear program of action before taking the first step into any venture. You should place your goals before and device a program of action to make it a reality. Refusing to sit down first to plan will make you re-sit. Re-sit is a polite way of informing you that you failed. Hence, you need to always think before acting.

Count the cost

As you sit down, you don't fold your hands. You sit down to map out what is needed to accomplish the goal set before you. The word 'count' means to analyze. Asses your expected goals on the scales of your present position and then set up strategies to balance them and meet up with your future. Planning will help you narrow down problems and solve them without stress.

Get facts

Uncommon planners hunt for uncommon facts. Facts are the raw material for planning. The strength of your plan is a function of the facts available to you. You must be well informed to be a good planner. There are several ways you access facts. You either get facts from above, by divine insight, through observation or research. You learn from good and bad experiences. The good ones motivate you to pursue your goals with full confidence while the bad ones teach you what not to do. It is better we learn from the mistake of others.

Think

Your facts will remain in their raw and unproductive state until you process them through productive thinking. You only utilize knowledge through thinking. If any lesson must become applicable to life, it must pass through the process of thinking.

Write down your plans

Planning is a combination of thinking and writing. By thinking, you search out what you desire to do; by writing, you arrest your thoughts. Writing makes your plans documented. Jesus was so particular about the issue of writing, that He instructed John ten times in the book of Revelation to write.

Commit your plans to God and trust Him for direction

Trust in the Lord with all your heart, and lean not on your own understanding; in all your ways acknowledge Him, and He shall direct your paths Proverbs 3: 5-6

Habakkuk 2:2 states we write down and make it plain. To make it plain means to make the journey clear. We must depend solely on God to make our plans successful.

There are several areas of your life that you must plan to achieve the desired success. They include planning your life, energy, resources, finances and materials, work and even your speech. You must mix your plans with faith for it to yield the desired result.

CHAPTER FOURTEEN

IDEAS

Ideas are plans, thoughts or suggestion especially about to do in a particular situation. It is a conception in the mind of something to be done; a plan for doing something, an intention. Ideas are pictures or impression in your mind of what somebody or something is like. It also means the aim or purpose of something. Mike Murdock renders it this way; **as a thought divinely planted by God that could solve a problem for someone**.

Facts about ideas

- Ideas are birthed in thought provoking atmosphere
- Ideas are the substance for productivity
- Your creativity is a function of your ideas
- Ideas are the birth place of incredible knowledge
- Ideas can make or mar you. So you must screen the ideas that come to you
- Ideas have the capacity of relocating you from the prison to the palace. It happened to Joseph.
- Your custom and ideology is sponsored by your dominant ideas
- Knowledge is a collection of ideas and knowledge properly applied is wisdom. So ideas are the raw materials for knowledge and wisdom.
- Men of uncommon ideas are always in command. They are commanders of multitude
- Ideas produce wealth; wealth will produce servants for you Genesis 30: 25-43

- Words are idea containers. Your level of knowledge is known through the ideas contained in your words.
- The poor are void of wealth oriented ideas. The word **POOR** mean Passing over Opportunities Repeatedly. A poverty stricken fellow is one who continuously ignores or does not recognize opportunities
- Your mind is the ware house of ideas
- Ideas have wings and can fly away never to return, if you don't arrest them. You arrest thoughts by writing them down. Ideas will always come to a person who places value on them.
- No devil in hell can withstand the strength of a God-given idea. The wisdom of God dumbfounds devils
- Use your mind. Your mind is not your boss, but your servant. If you don't use it, it won't work for you
- A developed mind creates a developed destiny
- Money is the by-product of ideas. You don't need to pray for money. You solve problems to get it. The gravity of problems you solve determines the amount of money you command
- Do not allow your mind to be dormant because a dormant mind begets a dormant life.
- Ideas rule the world. Men of uncommon ideas are always in command. If you are void of ideas, you become a servant to the one who has.
- No man speaks, acts or does anything above his level of reasoning
- Ideas are upgraded from time to time to maintain relevance. The automobile companies among others upgrade their products continuously to meet contemporary needs. This requires uncommon ideas.
- Money flows freely toward ideas. Money is a reward for uncommon ideas
- Stop looking for followers. Access incredible ideas and a crowd will press after you
- Much sweating is a proof of absence of ideas
- Uncommon ideas are the short cut to uncommon wealth
- The reason for idleness and unemployment is traced to lack of ideas. Mice Monroe said a Chinese man told him that why they

grow more prosperous than most blacks is simple- when a Chinese man arrive a new place, he looks for business but the black man chooses to look for a job. Jobs don't pay like businesses
- Uncommon ideas break stagnancy. It breaks the backbone of poverty. What you know, you will master but what you don't know will enslave you
- Ideas are the dividing line between the rich and poor
- **Hard work without headwork leads to hardship**. Engage your mind before engaging your hands
- Uncommon ideas will increase your worth and wealth
- The quality of goods you produce and the service you render is a function of your mind where ideas are received and processed
- Ideas will propel you to the top
- People perish when they are void of ideas Hosea 4: 6
- The word of God contains mysterious ideas to empower the saints
- When you are word barren, you become idea barren
- Ideas are golden gates to change
- An idea from God doesn't only bless you, it also blesses nations
- According to Oral Robert, when God promised you more than you have room to receive in Malachi 3: 10, He was speaking of ideas, insight and concept
- Ross Perot, a famed billionaire once said "one good idea can enable a man to live like a king the rest of his life
- An uncommon idea can create a lifetime of provision
- Ideas are solutions that eliminate stress and increase enthusiasm and joy.

Sources of ideas

- God
- Observation of your environment
- Your experience and that of others
- Research (read books) 2Timothy 2: 15
- Meditation Joshua 1: 8
- Interaction and interviewing

- Your mentor

Why you need ideas

- For effective planning Luke 14: 28-30
- For effective time management Eccl. 3
- For balanced growth Luke 2: 40, 52
- To update oneself to maintain relevance Joshua 1: 8
- For excellence in business
- For a fulfilled marriage
- For church planning and organization
- For effective leadership
- For financial success
- For wealth creation

PART FOUR

THE REALM OF PROSPERITY

The realm of prosperity is real and you need to fulfill certain conditions to live there. You must know that whatever miracle you desire from God, there are conditions to fulfill. If you can do your part, God will always do His. God's will for you is prosperity. God has promised prosperity but it is your responsibility to turn His promises into a covenant platform for awesome proofs.

CHAPTER FIFTEEN

WHAT IS PROSPERITY?

The Random House Dictionary defines prosperity as a successful, flourishing, or thriving condition, especially in financial respects; good fortune. It is the state of being successful, especially in making money. It is a general state of wellbeing. Prosperity does not permit sickness.

Beloved, I pray that you may prosper in all things and be in health, just as your soul prospers 3John 1: 2

Prosperity in the kingdom covers the spirit, soul and body. That is when you are seen to be prosperous. According to Mike Murdock (2002), **prosperity is simply having enough of God's provision to complete His instruction in your life.** Prosperity is a powerful tool for God's work-evangelization. In spreading the gospel, the timing of Christ's return is even affected. Satan's period of operation can be shortened when believers use prosperity as a tool for kingdom advancement (Matthew 24: 14). Through our giving, missionaries are sent, Christian television and radio stations are established, churches are built and bibles and tracts are printed. The essence of prosperity is much more than a comfortable life, good cars and mansions. It is having enough of God's supply to complete His instructions for your life; enough of His provisions to accomplish His commands. Achievers work out God's principles of prosperity while losers wait for some "magic moment of luck".

CHAPTER SIXTEEN

PROSPERITY IS GODLY

The bible is unequivocally clear on prosperity.

- It is God's will for you to prosper 3John 1: 2
- Prosperity spreads the gospel faster while poverty closes down mission fields Zech. 1: 17
- Prosperity makes people choose a place while others are rejected because of poverty
- God gives us power to get wealth and does not expect us to backslide Deut. 8: 18
- The new birth connects you to great wealth 1Cor. 8: 9
- Salvation precedes prosperity Psalm 118: 25
- God wants all Pastors to have rich members just like Pastor Timothy had 1Timothy 6: 7
- When God called you to serve Him, He had greatness on His mind Gen. 12: 1-3
- God called you to give you a future and a hope Jeremiah 29: 11

So you see that prosperity is godly. It makes you look like God. The rich are assets to the kingdom but the poor are liabilities. Your prosperity gives God pleasure (Psalm 35: 27).

The Role of Men of God

Ministers of the gospel play critical roles in the prosperity of believers.

They are the agents of prosperity. They are Christ's ascension gifts to the church (Ephesians 4: 11- 13).

...believe in the Lord your God, and you shall be established; believe His prophets, and you shall prosper 2Chronicles 20: 20

So the elders of the Jews built, and they prospered through the prophesying of Haggai the prophet and Zechariah the son of Iddo... Ezra 6: 14

God is responsible for your establishment (2Chronicles 20: 20) and you are established in righteousness (Isaiah 54: 14). But your prosperity is released to you through the teaching, preaching and prophesying of men of God. It follows therefore that a pastor who is not preaching and prophesying prosperity to his pew, is raising poverty-stricken believers who will end up as liabilities in the kingdom.

Why Certain Pastor's are Poor

The poverty of ministers is basically a mindset rooted in deliberate ignorance which many have accepted from erroneous teachings. Those who attack fellow ministers for preaching prosperity to believers are ignorant. After the attack, they still go around in need of money to do God's work. How can an unpowered pew finance the work when they are also in need of a savior? It is the will of God to make saviors out of us (Obadiah 1: 21). You cannot rise above your mindset. Every minister is a gift from Christ to His people to equip them for the work of the ministry. God's thought and ways are higher than man's (Isaiah 55: 9). Therefore follow after what he says in the word.

Now acquaint yourself with Him and be at peace... Job 22: 21

"Acquaint" in King James means to agree. When you agree with what God is saying from the scripture above, you will experience the following

    a)   God will come to you (vs. 21)
    b)   You will be built up (vs. 23)
    c)   You will lay gold as dust (vs. 24)

d) You will have plenty of silver (vs. 25)
e) You will become a financial wonder and a man of immeasurable authority (vs. 28)

This is what you stand to enjoy when you preach and prophesy prosperity to your pew. Of course you should know that if your members don't prosper and have money, your vision will suffer. When your members are poor, you will be the most affected, because it will show in your entire life. The vehicle that transports vision into the world is money. The scripture says where there is no vision; the people perish (Prov. 28: 18). But vision without resources to implement it, will suffer and be frustrated. Broken visions can cause devastation to the visionary. You need resources to bring your vision bare. These resources will come from the people you develop through insightful teachings and power packed prophesies.

Poor pastors have the temptation of worshipping the very few rich members they have. This ensnares them, which evidently lead to backsliding. We must provide direction for them to serve God with their breakthroughs. Teach them Luke 5: 8; Peter came to kneel before Jesus with his breakthrough. They should do same; they should not be high minded; they should trust not in their riches but to be rich in good works (of distribution) and remember that the Pastor is higher than the richest man in the congregation.

Why Pastors Must Preach Prosperity

- Faith comes by hearing:

So then faith comes by hearing and hearing by the word of God Romans 10:17

The quality of the word they hear forms the bedrock of the quality of prosperity they command. It is your duty to teach them because the word says

...how shall they hear without a preacher? Romans 10: 14

- It is God's will that we prosper 3John 1: 2
- We are commanded to teach even the rich in our congregation 1Timothy 6:7

- Jesus was anointed to preach the gospel to the poor Luke 4: 18
- So your God given visions can be fulfilled
- To fasten the spread of the gospel in preparation of Christ return Zech. 1: 17
- When your members prosper, you will also prosper
- Pastors have divine mandate to make many rich. It is a serious assignment that you must fulfill

...as poor, yet making many rich...2Cor. 6: 10

Don't say you are not yet rich, so that the preaching of kingdom prosperity is a no go area. No, the word says "as poor, yet making many rich". As you search the scriptures and discover truths, it will also make you free (John 8: 32). Make them rich and you will end up rich (Prov. 27: 23-27). If you are dependent today, God shall make you dependable tomorrow if you properly equip, encourage and guide your members to greatness.

- God wants the saints to be kingdom pillars and funders of the great commission. You need to make them know this.
- You are to prophesy prosperity on your members so they can prosper 2Chronicles 20: 20

How should Pastors go about this?

Teach practical steps to prosperity. The root of prosperity is in teaching Isaiah 48: 15-17. You need to learn. What you hear, learn and meditate upon, has a lot to do with what you end up with. The word, your imagination and action has the power to attract prosperity to you (Joshua 1: 8). Teach your pew the following

- God's will is prosperity 3John 1: 2
- His will is to spread the gospel through prosperity Zech. 1: 17
- Teach them joyful labor prov14:23,1Thess. 4: 11, 12; 2Thess. 3: 10-16. There is dignity in labor Deut. 28: 8, 12. God blesses what your hand is doing.
- Idleness and laziness is evil Prov. 6: 6, 10; Matt. 20: 1-8; Amos 6: 1. God doesn't bless lazy people.
- Dynamics of money flow. Money flows in the direction of goods and services Prov. 24: 26. When you provide right answers, you will attract money.

- Tithing and first fruit Lev. 27: 30, 31; Mal. 3: 10, 18; Prov. 3: 9-10
- To be rich towards God in their offering (Luke 6: 38, Mal. 1: 6, 8), their seeds (2Cor. 9: 10) and love offering (2Cor.9: 7)
- Teach vows, pledges and seeds 1Samuel 1: 11, Psalm 5: 14-15
- Obedience to the prompting of the Spirit Gen. 22: 1-17
- Honor God's servants and Prophets Gen. 14: 18-20; 18: 1, 10; 2Kgs 18: 36; Matt. 10: 40-42
- Teach them savings culture Gen. 44: 34-37; Matt. 25: 1-9
- Wise investments Eccl. 11: 1-4. He that has no savings and investments has no future Prov. 6: 6-10
- Teach them multiple streams of income Prov. 31: 10-31
- Teach money dynamics

  -Financial education

  -Assets and liabilities

  -Practical money management for financial freedom

  -Frugality. Refuse extravagance, spend money wisely and reasonably

  -Deliberate qualities, quantities, regular seed sowing on good grounds to attract divine blessing

  -Build career that have great future

- Prophesy prosperity on your members Ezra 6: 4; 2Chronicles 20: 20
- Teach them to focus on heaven, kingdom of God, fear of God and righteousness. As they do these, God will make the blessing to follow them Matt. 6: 33 and Psalm 1: 1-3, Psalm 23.

CHAPTER SEVENTEEN

WHY GOD PROSPERS HIS PEOPLE

God will never do anything or give you an instruction without a reason. There are scriptural reasons why God prospers His children. The following are note worthy

Our Prosperity Gives God Pleasure

...Let the Lord be magnified, who has pleasure in the prosperity of His servant Psalm 35: 27

All things exist to give God pleasure. Our prosperity gives Him pleasure. A loving father feels glad and accomplished when his offspring is doing well. So also does God feel whenever His children storm into prosperity. **Your prosperity is God's pleasure but your poverty is His pain**. Just as your faith in God please him, so also does your prosperity.

So You Can Be a Blessing

And I will make you a great nation, I will bless you and make your name great; and you shall be a blessing Genesis 12: 2

God's motivation for blessing you is so that you can be a blessing to others. The level of blessing God releases to you is a function of how ready you are to be a channel to reach others. The blessings of God come with a responsibility on your part to become a blessing to others. When you are tight-fisted, life becomes tight financially. Nothing comes into a hand that is closed. No tight-fisted person can handle the blessing. You only qualify for it when you are open-handed. Remember that whatever you have was given to you by God. It simply shows that we are first receivers before we become givers. The purpose it was given to you is so that you can in turn extend a helping hand to others. Learn from the farmers. Every successful farmer sets aside seedlings before consuming his harvest. Your seed is your future. Whenever you eat your seed, you mortgage your future. According to Mike Murdock every seed that leaves your hand, goes into your future. It leaves your hand for a while but goes into your future to create for you a bountiful harvest.

Every income you receive should be divided into three- your tithe, your upkeep and your seed. When you eat your tithe, you will suffer tightness financially; when you eat your seed, you empty your tomorrow of harvest, and you know the harvest is always over and above your seed. God is committed to give seeds continuously to sowers but bread is given to eaters. Stop eating all of your future today. Those who eat their tomorrow today are constantly exposed to calamity and untimely death. See what the widow in Zarephath told Elijah when he asked her for food

...I do not have bread, only a handful of flour in a bin, and a little oil in a jar; and see, I am gathering a couple of sticks that I may go in and prepare it for myself and my son that we may EAT IT, and DIE1Kings 17: 12.

So you see that to eat your financial seed and any other seed is to be exposed to death financially and otherwise. You need to know the first personality you should learn to give to is God. Matthew 6: 33 say "seek first the kingdom of God…"

...You shall love the Lord your God with all your heart, with all your soul and with all your mind. This is the first and great commandment Matt. 22: 37-38

So, your giving goes first to God, and then to men around you. God's love is a giving love. Your giving reveals your love. Make sure you give God first before others around you.

Prayer Point: Lord I terminate stinginess. Make me a blessing so I don't run out of harvest.

So We Can Spread the Gospel

...My cities shall again spread out through prosperity...Zech. 1: 17

God blesses us primarily for His kingdom sake. We are blessed of God so we can take part in spreading His kingdom. When you keep your money away from God, it takes you far away from Him. To keep your riches from God is to keep it for your hurt (Eccl. 5: 13). The rich fool in the gospel of Matthew, died untimely because of his selfishness and greed. God is set to bless anyone who is kingdom minded. Those who sponsor the cause of the kingdom are the ones to command kingdom wealth. God is giving prosperity to reach out to unreached areas with the gospel. The church can only be effective in executing the great commission to the ends of the world through prosperity. We need money to purchase ministry materials, printing of bibles and tracts, engage internet services and lot more to keep up with the modern world and her challenging demands. Prosperity will enhance the opening of new mission fields and the release of prepared and packaged missionaries but poverty closes up mission fields.

So We Can Build His House

Now, my son, may the Lord be with you; and may you prosper, and build the house of the Lord your God...1Chronicles 22: 11

You are prospered by God to build the house of God. People who are committed to building of God's house command the undistracted attention of God. In Luke 7 we see the story of a Centurion who caught the quick attention of Christ despite busy schedule. This is the testimony given to Jesus about the man and why Christ did not hesitate but to respond immediately;

And when they came to Jesus, they begged him earnestly, saying that the one for whom he should do this was deserving, "for he loves our nation, and has built us a synagogue." Luke 7: 4-5

When you read through the account of Israel in the book of Exodus, you will discover one profound reason why God blessed Israel before they left Egypt was to build His house.

And the Lord had given the people favor in the sight of the Egyptians, so that they granted them what they requested. Thus they plundered the Egyptians. Exodus 12: 36

And Moses spoke to all the congregation of the children of Israel, saying, "this is the thing which the Lord commanded, saying: "take from among you an offering to the Lord. Whoever is of a willing heart, let him bring it as an offering to the Lord: gold, silver, and bronze...then everyone came whose heart was stirred, and everyone whose spirit was willing, and they brought the Lord's offering for the work of the TABERNACLE of meeting, for all its service... Exodus 35: 4, 5 and 21

The Lord takes pleasure and is glorified when His children in obedience, commit their resources and time in building for Him.

"Go up to the mountains and bring wood and build the temple, that I may take pleasure in it and be glorified," says the Lord. Haggai 1: 8

The book of Haggai chapter one reveals why some Christians in church are not being blessed of God. They suspect family members and many others for their inability to prosper. Little do they know that God is the one fighting them for their lack of commitment towards the building of His house. There are some of such people who stay off from church on days when funds are raised for church projects. They feel they are playing smart but God cannot be mocked. We are blessed to also build God's house.

So You Can Provide For Your Family

God desires to prosper you to enable you provide for your family's needs. It is enshrined in the scriptures that we must provide our family's material and spiritual needs. Failure to live up to this, tantamount to denying the faith and it is said that such individual is worse than an infidel.

> *But if anyone does not provide for his own, and especially of those of his household, he has denied the faith and is worse than an unbeliever 1Timothy 5: 8*

God wants you so blessed that the blessing spreads to your second and third generation. The bible calls the man who leaves inheritance for his grand children, a good man.

> *A good man leaves an inheritance for his children's children... proverbs 13: 22*

God prospers you to care for your parents. Certain people give unfounded excuses why they don't care for their parents. They give such excuses as witchcrafts and inability on the part of their parents to care for them in the past. There are no conditions attached in the bible to the command of honoring one's parent but there is a promise attached for obedience.

> *Honor your father and mother, which is the first commandment with promise Ephesians 6: 2*

When you care for your parents, God becomes committed to your welfare and longevity of life on earth.

> *That it may be well with you and you may live long on the earth Ephesians 6: 3*

God wants you and your family to have plenty and to spare. He does not take delight in your poverty.

So You Can Give To the Poor

The first issue Christ addressed after He was anointed in Luke 4 verse 18 was preaching the gospel to the poor. So one reason God blesses us with riches and wealth is to help the poor. Christians who help the poor shall receive commendation.

> *For I was hungry and you gave Me food; I was thirsty and you gave*

Me drink; I was a stranger and you took Me in; I was naked and you clothed Me; I was sick and you visited Me; I was in prison and you came to Me; Then the righteous will answer Him, saying, Lord, when did we see You hungry and feed You, or thirsty and gave You drink? When did we see you a stranger and take you in, or naked, and clothe You? Or when did we see you sick, or in prison, and came to You? And the king will answer and say to them, 'Assuredly, I say to you, inasmuch as you did it to one of the least of these My brethren, you did it to Me Matthew 25:35-40

The poor around you are golden ticket to divine increase in life. There is always somebody in need located close to you. They are there to grant you a God-given opportunity to climb to your next level.

For you have the poor with you always...Matthew 26: 11

You are commanded to extend a helping hand to them as you can see below

For the poor will never cease from the land; therefore I command you, saying, you shall open your hand wide to your brother, to your poor and your needy, in your land Deuteronomy 15: 11

You must remember that giving to the poor is a commandment. The bible passage below buttresses this fact the more

He who keeps the commandment keeps his soul, but he who is careless of his ways will die. He who has pity on the poor lends to the Lord, and He will pay back what he has given Proverbs 19: 16-17

It is a grave danger to pay deaf ears to the cry of the poor. This is instructive

Whoever shuts his ears at the cry of the poor will also cry himself and not be heard Proverbs 21: 13

Those who want to be great must fulfill the condition of giving. Those who give to the poor will not lack. One of the secrets of Job's wealth revealed in the bible was giving to the poor. This was what he said in Job

29: 15-17

I was eyes to the blind, and was feet to the lame. I was a father to the poor, and I searched out the case that I did not know. I broke the fangs of the wicked, and plucked the victim from his teeth

Job was a force to be recon with in his days and he earned his place in plenty by fulfilling the commandment of giving to the poor. It is not enough to profess love to those in need. Your love must find expression in giving to meet someone's need.

The reasons briefly explained above are why God blesses His people. If these are the reasons you desire to prosper, get ready because God who searches the heart and knows the intents of men is so ready to bless you.

CHAPTER EIGHTEEN

CONDITIONS FOR PROSPERITY

Whatever God will do for you, there are conditions you must fulfill. No miracle comes your way until you are able to do your part. God won't do for you what has been committed to you. This is the reason miracles are worked out. God is a God of conditions. He is an "if" God.

Now it shall come to pass, IF you diligently obey the voice of the Lord God, to observe carefully all His commandments which I command you today, that the Lord your God will set you high above all nations of the earth Deut. 28: 1

IF they obey and serve Him, they shall spend their days in prosperity, and their years in pleasures Job 36: 11

IF you are willing and obedient, you shall eat the good of the land Isaiah 1: 19

So you see from the preceding passages that there are conditions attached to any blessing you seek. What qualify you for the blessing are the conditions you are able to keep. There are too many promises of God in the scriptures to His children, but these promises are turned into covenant platforms for unusual blessings, when you fulfill the conditions attached to them. Same applies to prosperity. Let's discuss few of them

Return

The first condition to securing divine wealth is in returning to God.

Until you return, your condition will not turn around. The prodigal son in the book of Luke had his worst condition turned around only when he returned to his father. Things won't stop turning against you until you return to God.

...return to me and I will return to you, says the Lord of hosts Mal.3: 7

There is too much to enjoy when you return. Let's see how the blessings are enumerated in Job 22 from 23 through 29

If you return to the Almighty:

- You will be built up
- Iniquity loses its power over you
- You become so rich in gold to the point that you begin to lay them in dust
- You will possess precious stones
- The Almighty will be your gold and silver
- You'll have joy unspeakable
- Consistent answers to your prayers
- God will illuminate your path
- You shall experience continuous lifting in the midst of adversity

These are not fabricated but are the sure promises of God to him who will fulfill His condition of returning whole heartedly. When the prodigal son returned, his status, dressing and diet changed. God is saying to you:

My son, give me your heart, and let your eyes observe my ways Prov. 23: 26

The Platform of Obedience

God loves you so much and He is so faithful that He cannot afford to mislead you. Whatever instruction He gives to you is aimed at giving you a future and a hope (Jeremiah 29: 11). God desires that you trust Him enough to obey Him.

The law of the Lord is perfect...and in keeping them there is great reward Psalm 19: 7-11

So you see that there are great rewards reserved for the obedient. Hear this:

If they OBEY and serve Him, they shall spend their days in prosperity and their years in pleasures Job 36: 11

Do you really desire to spend your days and years on earth in prosperity and pleasure? Fulfill the condition of obeying God. He prefers your obedience to your sacrifices.

...Behold, to OBEY is better than sacrifice, and to heed than the fat of rams 1Samuel 15: 22

If you must live, multiply and possess the land which the Lord vowed to deliver to you, obey His instructions.

Every commandment which I command you today you must be careful to observe, that you may live and multiply, and go in and possess the land of which the Lord swore to your fathers Deut. 8: 1

At the marriage feast in Cana, Mary the mother of Jesus instructed the servants in the feast to obey whatever the Lord commands, to secure their needed testimony.

...whatever He says to you, do it John 2: 5

There is more anointing in obedience than in sacrifice. Those who are committed to obeying God, command supernatural blessings in very cheap ways. The rod of Moses will very easily turn into a weapon of mass destruction in a consistent atmosphere of obedience. Deuteronomy 28: 1-13 opens to us the blessings of obeying God.

God's word is stronger than your intellect and your expertise. It is stronger than any economy. It is superior to any climate. Those who depend on their education or expertise will have problems obeying God (Luke 5: 1-7). As long as Peter kept analyzing the evident circumstance around him, he couldn't obey the Lord's command; this kept him still stranded until he quit leaning on his expertise and leaned on the word, was he able to take delivery of the blessing of a great catch. Your destiny will manifest on the platform of obedience. Obedience is more profitable than sacrifices. You only eat the good of the land when you are obedient to the almighty (Isaiah 1: 19).

The Platform of Service

If they obey and SERVE Him, they shall spend their days in prosperity and their years in pleasures Job 36: 11

No service rendered unto God goes unrewarded, none. Hebrews 11: 6 reveals God as a rewarder. The truth is that all of us are called to serve God and this we are admonished to do in spirit and in truth. Galatians 5: 13 inform us that by love, we should serve one another.

In the book of Exodus, we see Moses repeatedly speaking the mind of God to Pharaoh.

...Let my people go, that they may serve Me Exodus 8: 1, 20; 9: 1, 13; 10: 3

Before Jesus ascended to heaven, He charged His disciples with the service of preaching the gospel to sinners and teaching new converts to observe and do His will. Their relevance was embedded in this task. When they began this service, they rose from obscurity to prominence. Greatness comes through service. In the kingdom, only those with the servant heart ascend into great heights.

And whoever desires to be first among you let him be your slave just as the Son of Man did not come to be served, but to serve...Matthew 20: 27, 28

The kingdom way into an unhindered life of honor is in sincere service to God.

...if anyone serves Me, him My Father will honor John 12: 26

Your heart felt service is the currency that secures for you a place in the heart of God. In Acts 10: 4 an angel of the Lord visited Cornelius to inform him that his services have come up for a memorial before God. This brought a spiritual turn around for him and his entire household. Your service to God will not only profit you but all who are connected to you.

And let us not grow weary while doing good, for in due season we shall reap if we do not lose heart Galatians 6: 9

The Giving Platform

Giving is the tangible evidence of your victory over greed. It is the only guaranteed cure to greed. The worldly perspective of prosperity is measured by how much you have but it is not so in the kingdom. In the kingdom, prosperity is determined by how much you give. **Satan is a taker but God is a giver** (John 10: 10). Giving is godly

For God so loved...that He gave...John 3: 16

The proof of your love is evidenced in your giving. How much you love God is determined by how much you give or are willing to give to Him.

And Solomon loved the Lord...Solomon offered a thousand burnt offerings on that altar 1King 4: 3, 4

In Mike Murdock's words your offering is evidence that you possess:

- **A generous heart (willingness to share);**
- **A thankful heart (willingness to remember);**
- **A faith-filled heart (willingness to trust);**
- **A confident heart (willingness to expect).**

Your money is your ambassador. It represents you. It is your sweat, time, energy, toil and mental abilities. It is a major part of you, your power part. With it you exchange your way through life. You need money to trade it for food, shelter, clothing, education etc. The only way you can prove to your loved ones that you care about them is through your provision. As important as money is to you, when you give it to God, you publicly express that He is important to you. You demonstrate your faith to God when you release your money to Him.

Your giving to God ignites an exchange principle.

- When you give your sins to Him, He gives you forgiveness (1John 1: 9)
- When you give your confused mind, He gives you peace of mind (John 14: 27)
- When you give your unclean heart, He gives you a new one (Ezekiel 36: 26)
- When you release what you have, He releases what He has for you (Luke 6: 38)

In the kingdom, whatever leaves your hand does not leave your life, but goes ahead of you into your future to create a glorious future for you. It simply means that whenever you withhold from giving, you compromise your blessed future. Your giving is your love in action. Godly giving is to express our appreciation (Proverbs 17: 8). God treasures givers. Remember that everyone has a need to give (Matthew 10: 8). Also everyone has something to give (1Peter 4: 10). God expects you to give what you have, not what you don't have.

Giving is living but when you hold back from giving you start dying. No matter how little you have, when you engage the principle of giving, you place a demand on God to activate the life of abundance. The story of Elijah and the widow of Zarepha this instructive.

He (Elijah) called to her and said, please bring me a morsel of bread in your hand. So she said... I DO NOT HAVE BREAD, only a handful of flour in a bin, and a little oil in a jar, and see, I am gathering a couple of sticks that I may go in and prepare it for MYSELF and MY SON, that WE MAY EAT IT AND DIE 1kings 17: 11, 12

Notice that when her thought was centered on herself and son, poverty and death had legal grounds to take her and her son. But the story was not meant to be so. Elijah opened her eyes to the truth in God about giving saying

> *... The bin of flour shall not be used up, nor shall the jar of oil run dry (when you engage the giving law), until the day the Lord sends rain on the earth 1kings 17: 14*

The widow sacrificed poverty and death in exchange for abundance and life when she engaged the giving law. There are certain things you are holding onto that are meant to be given out to allow God release His unprecedented blessing on you. For you to go up there are certain things you must give up. Your due season for God's blessing is earned on the giving covenant platform. Until you are able to fill your heaven, there is no release of the blessing. Whatever discourages you from giving is a threat to your glorious release.

> *And let us not grow weary while doing good, for in due season we shall reap if we do not lose heart Galatians 6: 9*

There is what is called **due season.** It speaks of the time of your blessing. Your season is your time of fruitfulness. You may be asking, "When is my due season?" your season comes when your cloud is full.

> *If the clouds are full of rain, they empty themselves upon the earth... Ecclesiastes 11: 3*

Who is responsible in filling your financial cloud? It's no one else but you. All the earth does to receive rain from the cloud is to fill the cloud with water through evaporation and transpiration. When the cloud becomes full and heavy, it releases rain to earth. This also applies to us. We are to fill our financial cloud with all manner of giving. So we create our season through our giving. How fast or slow your season comes is determined by your measure of giving. There is no time to rest in giving. There are those who are in an endless season of financial rain because they keep filling their clouds even though it is full and is raining on them. Nothing will stop your clouds from releasing the blessing when they are full, nothing. **If nothing is going up from you, nothing will come down for you**. The fear of losing what you have is the reason you are losing what God has for you. Notice when evaporation is taking place, the earth gets drier and drier; but suddenly when condensation takes place and the clouds can no longer contain its weight, it pours down on earth and creates seasons of refreshing. Let us not be deceived, **your due season is not a function of prayer but of giving**. Beloved, you don't wait for your due season; you program your due season by deliberately giving sacrificially to fill up your cloud.

The Wisdom Platform

Wisdom is paramount in the pursuit of life's endeavors. It is the principal thing in life.

Wisdom is the principal thing; therefore get wisdom, and in all your getting, get understanding Proverbs 4: 7

Wisdom is the master key to all life's treasures. King Solomon got his unbelievable wealth on the wisdom platform. God spoke to Solomon these words:

… because you have ask this thing (wisdom), and have not asked long life for yourself, nor have asked riches for yourself, nor have asked for the life of your enemies, but have asked for yourself understanding to discern justice, behold, I have done according to your words… and I have also given you what you have not asked: both riches and honor, so that there shall not be anyone like you among the kings all your days 1kings 3: 11-13

Wisdom will grant you unhindered access to unending riches and honor. Hear what wisdom says in Proverbs 8 verses 18 and 19:

Riches and honor are with me, enduring riches and righteousness. My fruit is better than gold, yes, than fine gold, and my revenue than choice silver.

Where then can this wisdom be found? Job 28 and from verse 12 renders it thus:

But where can wisdom be found? And where is the place of understanding? Man does not know its value, nor is it found in the land of the living. The deep says, it is not in me; and the sea says, it is not with me. It cannot be purchased for gold, nor can silver be weighed for its price. It cannot be valued in the gold of Ophir, in precious Onyx or sapphire. Neither gold nor crysal can equal it, nor can it be exchanged for jewelry of fine gold. No mention shall be made of coral or quartz, for the price of wisdom is above rubies. The topaz of Ethopia cannot equal it, nor can it be valued in pure gold. From where then does wisdom come? And where is the place of understanding? It is hidden from the eyes of all living, and concealed from the birds of the air. Destruction and death say, we have heard a report about it with our ears. God understand its way, and He knows its place. God saw wisdom and declared it; He prepared it, indeed, He searched it out. And to man He said, behold, the fear of the Lord, that is wisdom, and to depart from evil is understanding.

Wisdom is the correct application of knowledge and this is found in no other man, place or thing but in God. The word of God is the wisdom of God in print, handed over to humanity to command divine wealth.

Access His Voice

Anyone in constant touch with God's voice enjoys sweat less success. The voice of God frees you from every doubt and fears of life. Apostle Paul was fearless in the midst of shipwreck because he heard from God. Elijah prospered in the midst of a severe faming in Israel because he heard from God.

Thenthe word of the Lord came to him (Elijah), saying, get away from here and turn eastward, and hide by the Brook Cherith, which flows into the Jordan. And it will be that you shall drink from the brook, and I have commanded the ravens to feed you there;... then the word of the Lord came to him, saying, arise, go to Zarephath, which belongs to Sidon, and dwell there. See, I have commanded a widow there to provide for you 1Kgs 17: 2-4, 9.

The passage is loaded with insight. Those who access the voice of the Lordprovoke divine direction and live under **His commanded blessings**.

Divine guidance and supernatural provisions are provoked under an open heaven where the voice of God is released. The voice of God breaks in pieces generational poverty. Note that there were many brooks in Israel but Elijah was given the name of a particular brook and its location. If Elijah had gone to the one his eyes and heart crave for, he would have missed out on the blessing. This is the problem with Christians today. They don't consult God before moving into a place, before and during marriage, or before buying a thing. This is the reason for many problems today. Lot lusted after and chose the lands of Sodom because his senses told him it was loaded with prospects but Abraham waited on God's voice. By the voice of God he found his place of the blessing. Today an average Nigerian longs to go abroad. Your provision is not from abroad but from above. Before Moses sent spies into the land of Canaan, he received the instruction from the Lord. What you possess and how far you possess it is a function of your hearing God.God told Abraham, as far as you can see from the north to south, east to the west, I have given to you.

Also note that Elijah secured God's voice in the place called "HERE" and the voice instructed him to go to the place called "THERE". There is a place in God called HERE and a place called THERE. Here is the place of His presence and voice while "there" is the place of provision.

And the Lord said, "Here is a place by me, and you shall stand on the rock Exodus 33:21

But as for you, stand here by me, and I will speak to you all the commandments, the statutes, and the judgments which you shall teach them... Deut. 5: 31

Those who access the place of God's voice are never stranded in their life's pursuit. King David fought about sixty six battles and suffered no defeat because he was constantly in touch with the voice of God. Your access to the place called 'Here' connects you to God's instruction to succeed in the place called 'There'. You obtain a prophesy 'Here' to live a fulfilled life 'There'. It is so important for Christians to seek and secure God's voice. It took Elijah forty day's journey to access the place of the still, small voice of God. Your appointed place to prosper is 'There' but you need conscious effort to secure God's instruction in the place called 'Here'.

When Naomi and her family left Bethlehem for Moab because of famine, she lost her husband and two sons simply because she moved without hearing His voice. Child of God! Go after His voice. He created places before he made people. He knows where you are to succeed. Abraham at 75years was unfulfilled until he heard God's matching order to leave where he was to Canaan (the place of his blessing). God made Adam and put him in the Garden of Eden (a place of prosperity). Ask Him to move you into your Eden. I see you getting there in Jesus precious Name.

The Work Platform

Work is not a curse; it is not a misfortune. It actually existed long before the curse was enacted.

Then the Lord God took the man and put him in the Garden of Eden to tend and keep it Genesis 2: 15

Man was not to waste or spend it but to tend and keep it. God does not want you to be a waster or spender of resources but a worker and keeper of resources. You just have to engage the work principle of God to prosper. Inheritance is no substitute for practical input. It does not enhance worth. There is a proverb that says that 'any child that depends on inheritance has given himself over to poverty. Inheritance is not a holder of destiny. I know a young boy who inherited lands and houses from his father. He switched into prodigality and as a result sold all his lands. When hunger came, he resorted to robbery which incidentally took his life. So you see, inheritance without a work mindset, gravitates towards poverty and misery.

Work promotes worth (Psalm 1: 3). What you have not worked for does not add to your worth. This is the undoing of those lazy people who are in quest of free money; money never earned. They therefore live very cheap lives that crash on any kind of rock. Your work today determines your throne tomorrow (Proverbs 22: 29). Your commitment to work determines your attainment in the world. Things will always work for those who work. Work is the solution to lack and penury. It is the gateway to all round fortune and the most effective physical fitness exercise. Every delightsome worker by covenant mystery lives a healthy life. You are God's temple and like every physical building, idleness makes your body system begin to rust and decay; and through idle hands begins to drop (Ecclesiastes 10: 18).

God blesses the work of our hands. Without work, there is nothing available for God to bless. He does not bless idle hands. He only blesses busy hands. Your wealth is in your work. Jesus hates the sight of idleness and He is committed to only reward workers. See what He says

... Why have you been standing here idle all day? They said to him, because no one hired us. He said to them, you also go into the vineyard, and whatever is right you will receive Matthew 20: 6, 7.

You only receive what is right (financial success) when you are busy doing something reasonable. Proverbs 28: 19 says he who tills his land will have plenty of bread. This simply means that hunger is the end result for idleness. Chapter 10 of Proverbs and verse 4 holds that he who has a slack hand becomes poor, but the hand of the diligent makes rich. No one is born poor, neither is anyone born rich. Every one of us came to this world stark naked. People arrive earth to become whatever they choose to be. Just as several people are becoming rich, so also are many becoming poor. It is a function of choice. It is the hand of the diligent that makes rich. This shows that the making of wealth is not limited to giving alone. While giving delivers to you the blessing, work opens the channel for the blessing to reach you. Your giving creates room for the blessing (Proverbs 18: 16) but your work introduces you to men of substance (Proverbs 22: 29).

The righteous is prospered via whatever he does (Psalm 1: 3) and not whatever he gives. God is ever committed to bless the works of your hands but where there is no work in your hand, there is nothing for Him to bless. There is no future for idle people in the kingdom. If you are not hard working, you automatically position yourself for a hard life. Those who feel work is a function of the curse are lacking in understanding. If God worked who are you not to do same? Genesis 2 and verse 8 tells us that God planted a garden eastward of Eden. In John 5 and verse 17, Jesus revealed that the Father has been working until now, and that he has been doing same. Wealth isn't for those who wish it but for those who work it out. Idle people are not qualified to eat (1Thes. 3:10). Let me conclude this by saying that your hard work without God tends to labor (Psalm 127: 1). Also your hard work without the giving covenant platform tends to frustration (Haggai 1:11).

Search and maximize Opportunities

Do not sleep, lest you come to poverty; open your eyes and you will be satisfied with bread Prov. 20: 13

The reason for poverty amongst many is because they walk about with closed eyes to opportunities. Only those with open eyes to opportunities will be satisfied with bread. Those with closed eyes go around looking for jobs. Some even take jobs that have no great future. They work for pea nuts and live by the saying "**half bread is better than none**". This is a poor man's mindset. It is unwise for a family man to take a driving job with a monthly remuneration of twenty thousand naira without other benefits. Some of these people work from morning till night for such peanuts. I have also seen family people taking teaching jobs of a monthly remuneration of ten to fifteen thousand. They are proud to have a white collar job but they are suffering in poverty. What future does this kind of jobs offer? Those with the rich mindset don't settle for crumbs. They viscously gun for opportunities to create wealth. Hear this: **when a person with a poverty mindset comes into a place, he seeks for a job but when he who has a rich mindset comes around, he looks for a business.**

God wants our eyes open to opportunities. Wherever you find yourself, there are certain things God wants you to look out for, if you must possess that land and prosper in it. He told Abraham to lift up His eyes and see (Gen. 13:14). Let's see Numbers 13:18-20

... See what the land is like: whether the people who dwell in it are strong or weak, few or many; whether the land they dwell in is good or bad; whether the cities they inhabit are like camps or strong holds;

whether the land is rich or poor; and whether there are forests there or not.

What is God opening our eyes to? Wealth is earned and not awarded. It is created. You must make conscious and deliberate efforts to become rich. The passage above educates us on certain vital issues to settle, if we must possess the land and prosper in it. These questions will help:

What are the strengths and weaknesses of the people?

Every settlement is created by her people. The needs of people drive them into various activities. God spoke to the Israelites through Moses in their bid to possess Canaan to find out the strengths and weaknesses of the people. What are they good at and what is their area of weakness? You rarely defeat a man in his area of strength. You don't command the attention of someone who knows how to do what you are doing very well. Don't ever anticipate having the patronage of people who know how to produce your product. That is their area of strength. Those who will come to you are those who need what you have but lack the ability to produce it. They will seek after you because that is their point of weakness. So God is telling us from the passage above that you can prosper when you know the weakness of the people around you. If you can fill in for their weakness, they will pay anything to get their needs met. This is the reason the developed world are doing better than the third world countries. Technology is their point of strength, so they come to developing countries that are weak in the area. Financial success is attained where you are able to identify needs and proffer solutions to them.

Are the People Few or Many?

The population of people in an area tells to a great extent if a business will thrive or not. When Jesus instructed Peter to go lunch his net, he told him to go to the deep because you find more fishes in quantity and quality in the deep. In growing a church, the population of people in the region where the church is found is a factor to really consider. Knowing the population will give you an idea of the returns to anticipate. So God wants you to consider the number of people and balance it with the possible returns you envisage. The people from your market, so you must consider if what you are introducing in an area will need a larger or fewer population to be successful.

Is the Land Good or Bad?

A wise farmer ascertains the prospect of any land of interest before sowing his seeds. Sowing it in a bad land will only result to misery in the near future. God wants you to study the place of interest if it will support your investment or not. That's the reason certain investors avoid politically unstable societies. Is the target place for investment of your capital good and supportive or is it bad and a threat to your vision. This should be sorted out before investment begins.

What is the Nature of the Place?

Is the place a city, village or a sub-urb? Is it a camp? Is the place secured? Is the place prone to attacks or is it safe for investment? These questions are essential and God wants you to consider them in your bid to possess the land and prosper in it.

Is the Land Rich or Poor?

This prepares the mind of the investor on the place and people he is set to interact with. What abounds in the land and what is the area they are lacking? Your knowledge of the wealth or poverty of the land will arm you with useful information to improve on their status.

Is the Land Naturally Endowed?

In the passage, Israel was asked to find out if they have a forest or not. Your knowledge of the dominant natural resource will arm you with the kind of investment needed to embark upon. The natural resources in an area are the factors that determine the kind of people in the area as well as their dominant occupation.

You Need a Man

When God decides to help you, He passes through a man. This is because men are the signature of God. When He decides to help you, all He does is to endorse a man on your life. Also when the devil desires to destroy you, he uses a man as his instrument. No man is an Island. Even the Island requires the help of another land called valley. Men are the ladder to your great heights in life. Men are the raw materials to your financial success. Men are gates linking you to your next level. It is dangerous to be alone. Even God said:

It is not good that man should be alone; I will make him a helper comparable to him Genesis 2: 18

Every man has a God ordained helper, comparable to him. This does not give anyone clearance to put confidence in man. It leads to a cursed life.

Thus says the Lord: Cursed is the man who trusts in man and makes flesh his strength, whose heart departs from the Lord. For he shall be like a shrub in the desert and shall not see when good comes, but shall inhabit the parched places in the wilderness, in a salt land which is not inhabited Jeremiah 17: 5,6.

When you put confidence in God, you provoke the release of the blessing (Jeremiah. 17: 7, 8). There are God ordained helpers located at every junction of your life. Before Jesus started his ministry, God sent a helper ahead of Him.

There was a man sent from God, whose name was John. This man came for a witness, to bear witness of the Light that all through him might believe John 1: 6, 7.

When severe famine rocked both Egypt and Canaan to the point that money even failed (Genesis 47:15), God provided a man in the person of Joseph to save Jacob and his entire household, including Pharaoh and his kingdom.

You shall dwell in the land of Goshen, and you shall be near to me, you and your children, your children's children, your flocks and your herds, and all that you have. There I will provide for you, lest you and your household, and all that you have, come to poverty... Gen. 45: 10, 11

How early or late you get a miracle is the function of the kind of man you are connected to. The impotent man found at Bethesda pool said to Jesus:

... Sir I have no man to put me into the pool when the water is stirred up... John 5:7

So you see that your welfare is guaranteed when you have a well meaning helper. Let me open your eyes to five God ordained men you need in your life so you can lead a successful life.

Advertisers

It is advert that brings products from hiding into the hands of those in need of them. Every product in the store or warehouse is in the prison until it is introduced to consumers. No matter how talented or skillful you are in life, you need an advertiser to introduce you to people that matter. As anointed as Christ was when He was on earth, he was like a lone ranger until John the Baptist introduced Him as the Lamb of God that takes away the sins of the whole world. It was after the introduction that two disciples of John left him and began following Jesus. Joseph was gifted in interpretation of dreams but he remained in the prison until the butler in Pharaoh's palace introduced him to the king. For the two years that the butler forgot him, he remained in the prison with his gift. Your gift is not enough; you need an advertiser. Great men will only send for those that are recommended to them.

Then Pharaoh sent and called Joseph and they brought him quickly out of the dungeon; and he shaved, changed his clothing and came to Pharaoh Gen. 41: 14

What his gift could not do in two years, the power of advertisement did in just a moment. Advertisement is the cream that makes you appealing to men of substance. It rubs on you a compelling fragrance that makes the rich unable to resist you. Joseph was brought out from prison quickly and his freedom given back to him on a platter just because of an advertiser. Who is advertising you? The caliber of person advertising you determines your level of success and influence.

Financial Helpers

Life becomes a burden when you lack finances to execute your visions. When money is lacking to transport visions into reality, it brings about frustration and heart breaks. There are many in our societies who walk the streets in frustration yet with powerful ideas on their minds. We all need God ordained financial helpers to finance our ideas. Even Jesus the Christ had some women who committed their resources is sponsoring the cause of the gospel. Zachariah 1: 17 say the kingdom of God is enlarged through prosperity. Nehemiah's burden to rebuild the broken and fallen walls of Jerusalem became a reality when King Artaxerxes decided to help him. I see your financial helpers unable to rest until they fulfill the mandate of God in your life in Jesus name.

Burden Bearers

No one runs well and arrives destiny early when suppressed with burden. Hebrews 12: 1 says we should lay aside every weight. It is possible to die unfulfilled when you are carrying too much of life's burden. By divine design, Jesus was to die in Golgotha, but when he was distance away, the weight of the cross was so much that he could not go further. It was at that instance that Simon the Cyrenaic came to help Christ carry His cross to the place of His crucifixion. He was Christ's ordained burden bearer. Your burden bearers are graciously anointed to help you fulfill your destiny earlier than you would have done on your own. I see your burden bearers locating you in Jesus matchless name.

Destiny Directors

What ever you desire to venture into in life, there is a man succeeding there. The best person to consult is the person that knows more than you in the field you are venturing into. When David's family and that of his men were captured by his enemies, he was asked by God to pursue, overtake and recover all but was not told where to go. That was left in the hands of his God ordained director. When you get to your cross road where you do not know the next point of call, God graciously provides a man to give you direction. You shall never be stranded any more.

The Man Whose Oil Works for You

Mankind is controlled by altars. You are either connected to a divine altar or a satanic altar. Every altar is manned by a priest. Your deliverance, preservation and prosperity are made possible by God via the instrumentality of a Man of God.

By a prophet the Lord brought Israel out of Egypt, and by a prophet he was preserved Hosea 12: 13

... Believe the Lord your God, and you shall be established; believe His prophets, and you shall prosper 1Chronicles 20: 20

You need a man whose oil works for you to prosper and become a financial warlord. God wills to make you His kingdom financial pillar but you need a prophet who will provoke prosperity upon you through the vehicle of prophesy.

So the elders of the Jews built, and they prospered through the prophesying of Haggai the prophet and Zechariah the son of Iddo... Ezra 6: 14

Israel needed a king and by ancestral declaration, the scepter of leadership was never to depart from Judah; but by reason of the prophetic mantle on the life of Prophet Samuel, Saul a Benjamite became the first King of Israel (1Samuel 9).

There are however scriptural rules to taking delivery of the blessing in the life of your prophet.

- Receive your Prophet (Matthew 10: 41)
- Believe your Prophet (2Chronicles 20: 20)
- Obey your Prophet (John 2: 5)
- Respect your Prophet

By the anointing in the name of Christ Jesus, I bring to an end generational poverty in your life and family.

Apply Genesis 1: 28 Principles

Then God blessed them, and God said to them, be FRUITFUL and MULTIPLY; FILL THE EARTH and subdue it... Genesis 1: 28

The road to prosperity starts with the ability to **produce fruit**. Do you want to prosper financially? What can you produce? How relevant is the product to the needs of people? If you have a product to present, money will show its presence to you in a ground style. But producing a product is not just enough to bring the kind of money that will catapult you into tremendous riches. This takes us to the next stage.

The next stage is **multiplication** of the product. The single product on its own does not hold financial success; but when it is multiplied, it will benefit more people. Multiplying the product means multiplying the returns you would have gotten from a product. After multiplying it, you are then ready for the next stage.

The third stage speaks of your **ability to make the product reach the hands of those who need them**. Filling the earth speaks of your ability to distribute your product. It is at this point that money leaves the hands of people into your hands. Producing and multiplying your product alone holds no financial future until you develop modalities through which your product gets to the hands of many. Your dominion comes when you have been able to subdue, that is control your market.

Create multiple Streams of Income

Holding tenaciously to a single source of income is synonymous to laying all your eggs in a basket. Financial success is guaranteed when you move from depending on a single source of income to creating multi-streams of income. Even if you are an employee, you can still create other revenue points. The more revenue points you are able to create, the more inflow of money you command. Your welfare is threatened when you have a single source of income that is under pressure. But a man with several revenue points has no need to panic. Make your money work for you through investment.

Go for Assets

When you are not buying assets, you are buying liabilities. **Liabilities are those things that still take money out of your hand after acquiring them**. Whatever you keep spending money on after buying them which brings no income in return is a liability. Liabilities increase your propensity to spend and this leads to poverty. Those who command financial success acquire more and more assets. **An asset is that which increases your income flow**. Assets add and multiply your income. You need more assets to generate enough money to cater for some useful liabilities.

The purposes for which certain stuffs are acquired make them either an asset or liability. A car bought for commercial purpose is an asset but when bought for personal use, it becomes a liability. The rich will advise you to buy the car for commercial purpose because that way, you will have money to buy your personal car without stress. It also applies to building of houses. Houses built for personal use are liabilities since the owner spends much in maintaining it. But when houses are built for commercial purposes, they are assets. You are admonished to go for more assets before liabilities.

CHAPTER NINETEEN

YOUR TRUE FINANCIAL STATUS IN CHRIST

Let me conclude by reminding you that the work of Christ was the revelation of his grace to mankind which divinely qualified the unqualified. His substitutionary work transported mankind from the kingdom of darkness to His own kingdom (Colossians 1: 13). The manifestation of the grace of God removed us from the realm of poverty to the prosperity realm. Your new birth in Christ gave you a new identity. You are now rich and not poor. You need to understand this spiritual truth which cannot be broken.

For you know the grace of our Lord Jesus Christ that though He was rich, yet for your sakes He became poor, that you (I mean you) through His poverty might become rich. 2 Corinthians 8: 9

The phrase "**become rich**" brings you to the point of responsibility. This is good for you to know: **you are not the poor trying to get rich; you are the rich discovering your inheritance in Christ.** This is the clear gospel Christ meant when He said "to **preach the gospel to the poor**". This is the reason the Lord spoke in Ecclesiastes 10: 5-7 thus:

There is an evil I have seen under the sun, as an error proceeding from the ruler: Folly is set in great dignity, while the rich (you) sit in lowly place. I have seen servants (the unrighteous) on horses, while princes (the righteous) walk on the ground like servants.

If you are born again and you are still wallowing in poverty, it means you have not discovered your true identity. When the prodigal son came to himself, he took a bold step that gave him his true identity. You are not a slave; you are a king. When the Bible calls Christ the king of kings, it was referring to him as the king of believers. It is a grave error to live in poverty.

You are not poor. Circumstances around you may call you poor but that is not who God says you are. Your circumstance is not your conclusion. God has the final say over your life. See yourself in the light of God's word and discover what you have been ignorant of all this while. I see you bouncing back. I know who I am in Christ.

I close with this words to you: You are better than the food you are eating, the kind of clothes on you, the kind of house you live and the kind of live you are living. Say after me: I AM BETTER THAN THIS (say it again and again). You are the rich discovering your inheritance in Christ and not that poor stranded fellow. God bless you and see you at the top.

Shalom.

REFERENCES

David O. Oyedepo (2005):**Understanding Financial Prosperity**; Dominion Publishing House, Canaan Land, km 10, Idiroko Road, Ota, Ikeja, Lagos.

Mike Murdock (2002):**The Wisdom Commentary 1**; Word of Faith Publications/ stores; 20/30 Oba Market Rd. Benin City.

Kenneth Copeland (1974):**The Laws of Prosperity**; Kenneth Copeland Publications; Fort Worth, TX76192-0001.

Kenneth E. Hagin (2007):**Biblical Keys to Financial Prosperity.**Kenneth Hagin Ministries, Inc. Tuhbujlsa, OK74150-0128. USA.

Robert T. Kiyosaki et al (1998): **Rich Dad Poor Dad**. Warner Books, Inc. 1271 Avenue of the Americas, New York, NY 10020.

Sunday Adelaja (2009):**Money Won't Make You Rich; God's Principles for True Wealth, Prosperity and Success**; Charisma House, a Strang Company; 600 Rinehart Road, Lake Mary, Florida 32746.

T.D. Jakes (2005):**64 Lessons for a Life without Limits**. Simon and Schuster UK Ltd; 1st Floor, 222 Gray's Inn Road, London, WCIX 8H

A CALL FOR COMMITMENT

PARTNER WITH NKANU OVAI WORLD OUTREACH (NOWO)

OUR MANDATE: Appointed to declare the lifting of mankind

OUR MISSION: To spread the undiluted gospel of Jesus Christ across the nations of the world through evangelistic campaigns, seminars, conferences and visits to needy with signs and wonders following.

OUR MOTIVATION: …Go out into the highways and hedges and compel them to come in, that my house may be filled Luke 14: 23

Partner with us by sponsoring the work of God through weekly, monthly or yearly financial donations or other ways you are led by God to facilitate our God given mandate. God bless you.

Contact us on

+234(0)8063534539; + 234(0)8095971346

Or

Email: pastornkanu@gmail.com

ABOUT THE AUTHOR

Nkanu Ovia Nkanu is a dynamic minister of the gospel, serving with Assemblies of God Nigeria, Akamkpa District. He is the coordinator of Akamkpa District Youth Ministrues. He is the president and founder Nkanu Ovia World Outreach (NOWO), an interdenominational evangelistic organization commissioned to declare the lifting of men all over the world.
He is a preacher by calling and an evangelist by ministry, a motivational speaker, a revivalist, crusade speaker and a writer. He hails from Ebom community in Abi local government area, cross river state Nigeria. he is called and commissioned by God with a mandate to declare the lifting of men in his generation.
He is married to his lovely wife Neji Nkanu and their union is blessed with two wonderful sons – Ben Chris and Devine.

OTHER BOOKS BY THE AUTHOR

The book in your hand is life changing. It is for the Gideon of our generation who is asking "where are the miracles our fathers told us?"

Don't drop the copy in your hand, it is the answer you have been craving for. Read it and put into practice what you read. See you at the top, where the eagles are gathering. **Shalom.**

What is tithe? Is tithe optional or obligatory? Which is the correct way to tithe? Will my refusal to tithe stop me from going to heaven?

How can the tithe benefit my finances? What must I tithe? Are pastors exempted from tithing? Should a salary worker tithe his gross or net income? These and more questions shall this book be committed to answer, not excluding the consequences of not tithing as well as the benefits of tithing.

This book was born out of a deep desire for God to activate and charge the prayer and evangelical life of believers. It is challenging, educative, revealing, incisive, anointed and power packed. It is a healing balm to every facet of your life.